13

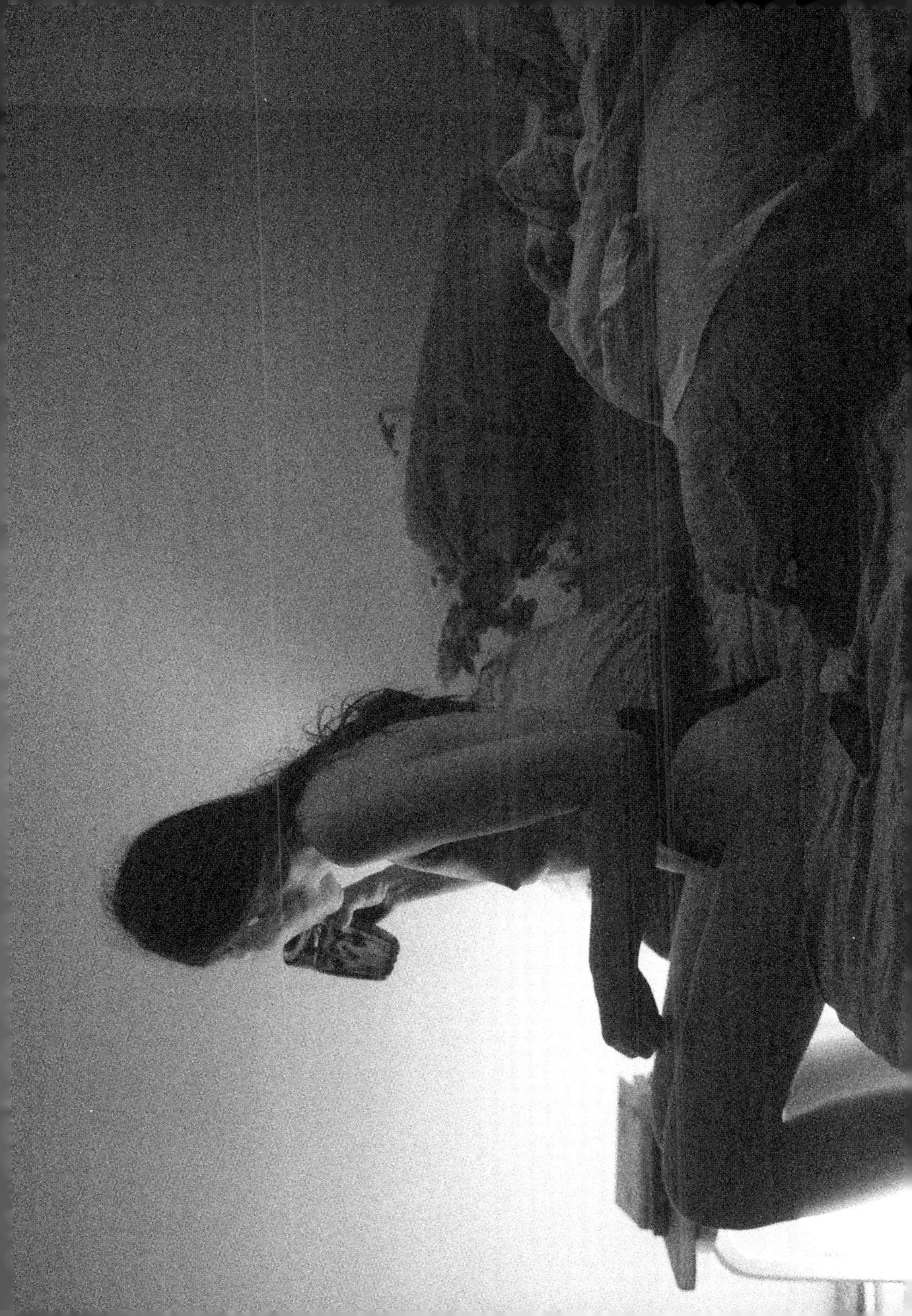

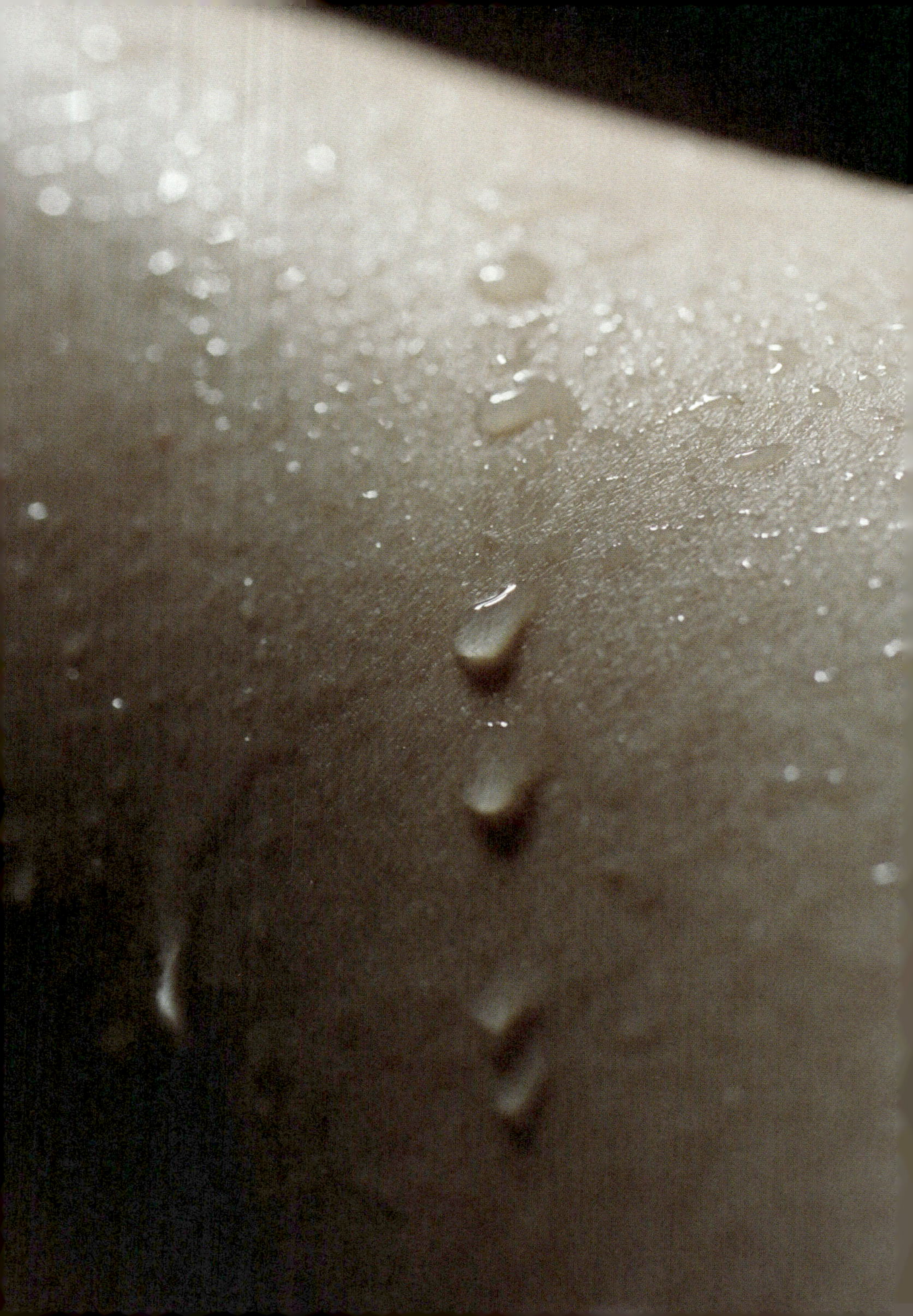

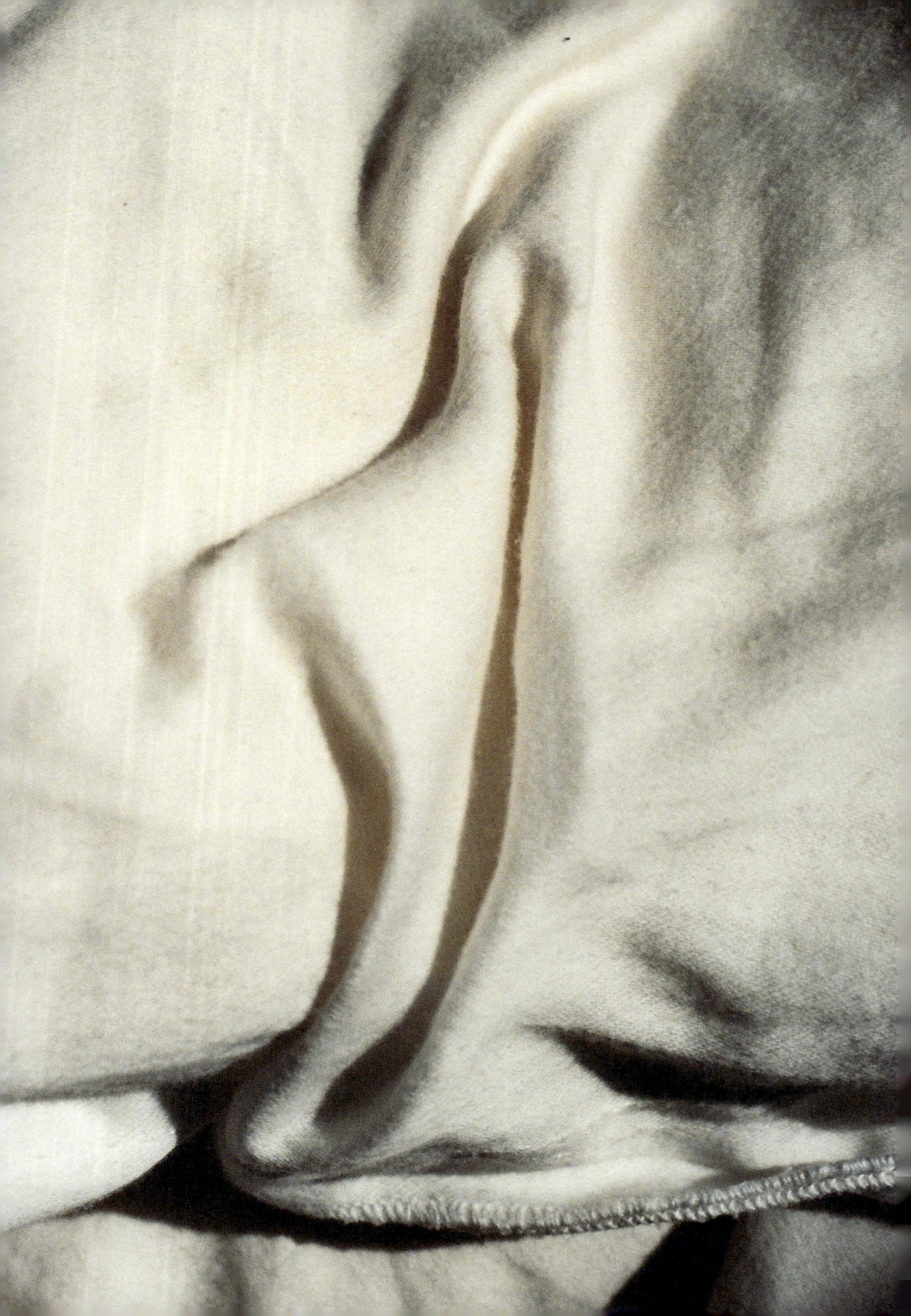

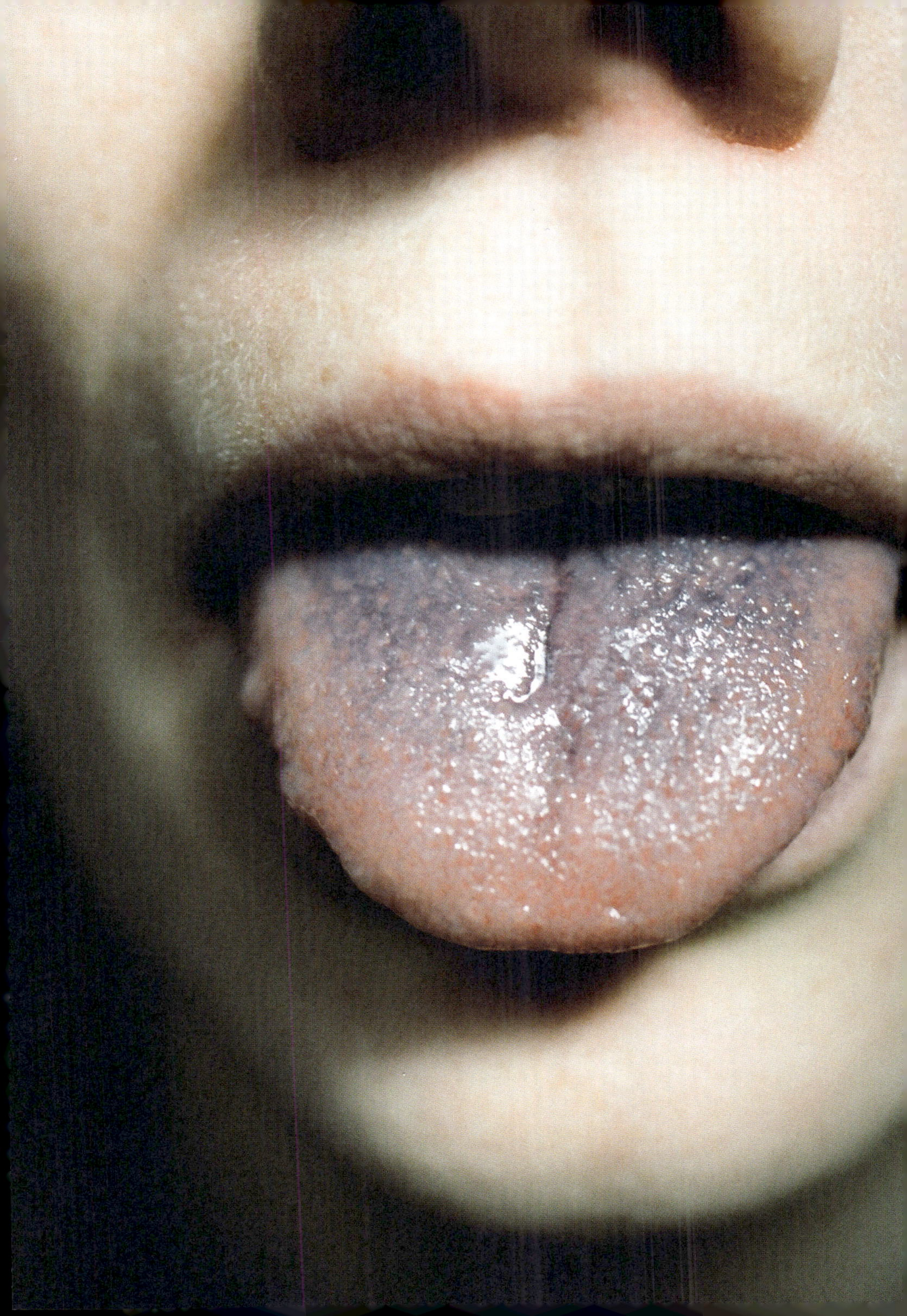

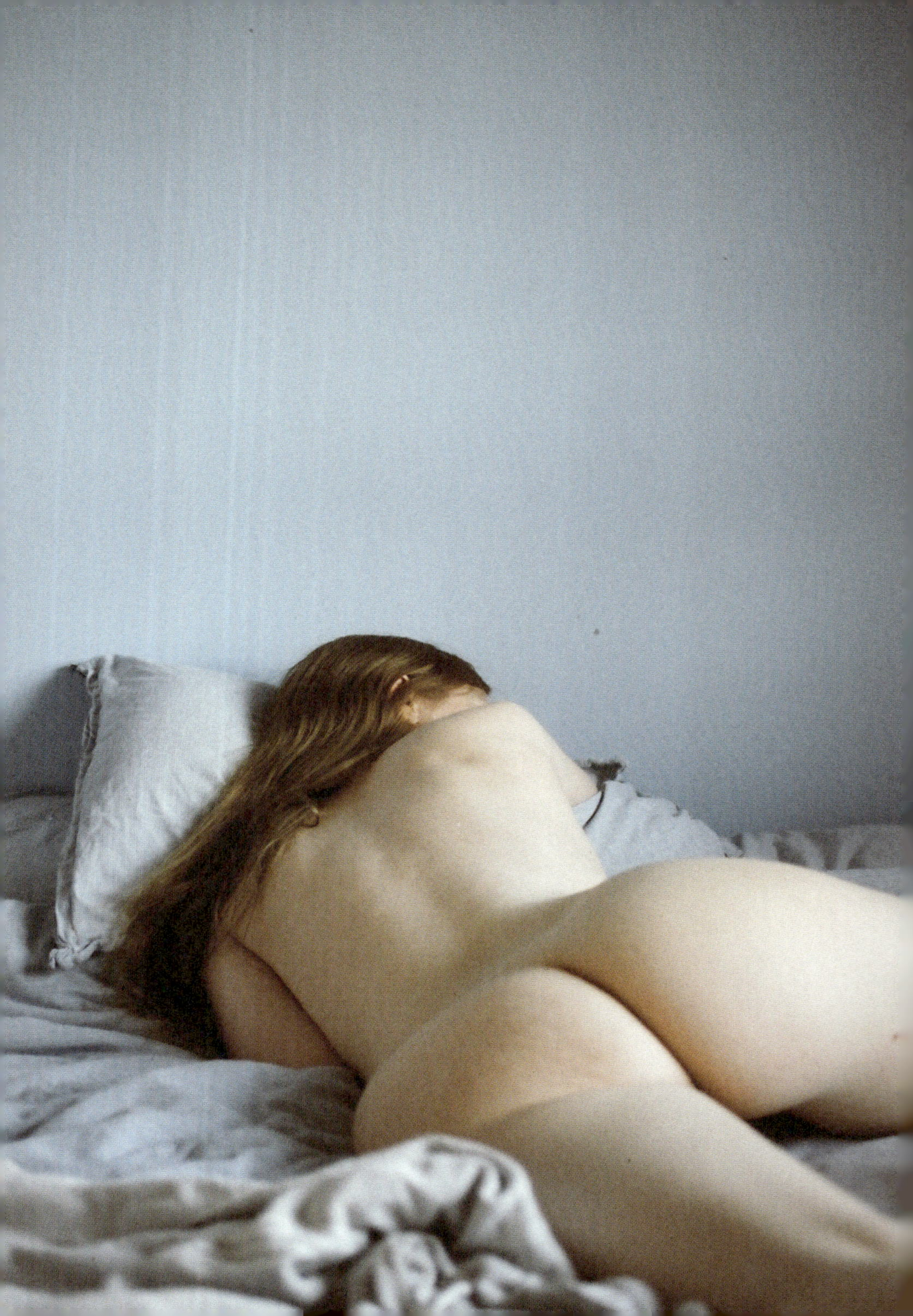

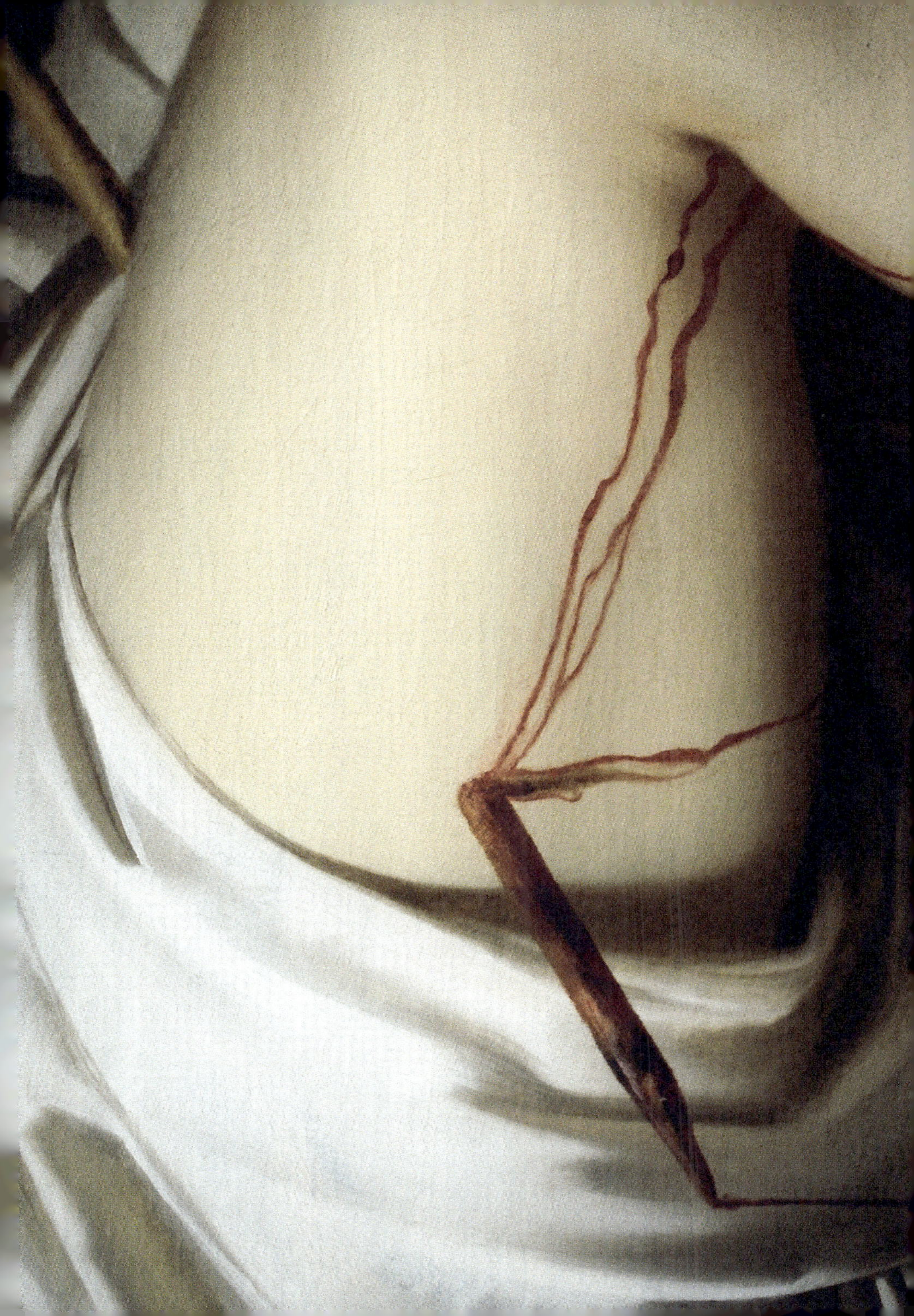

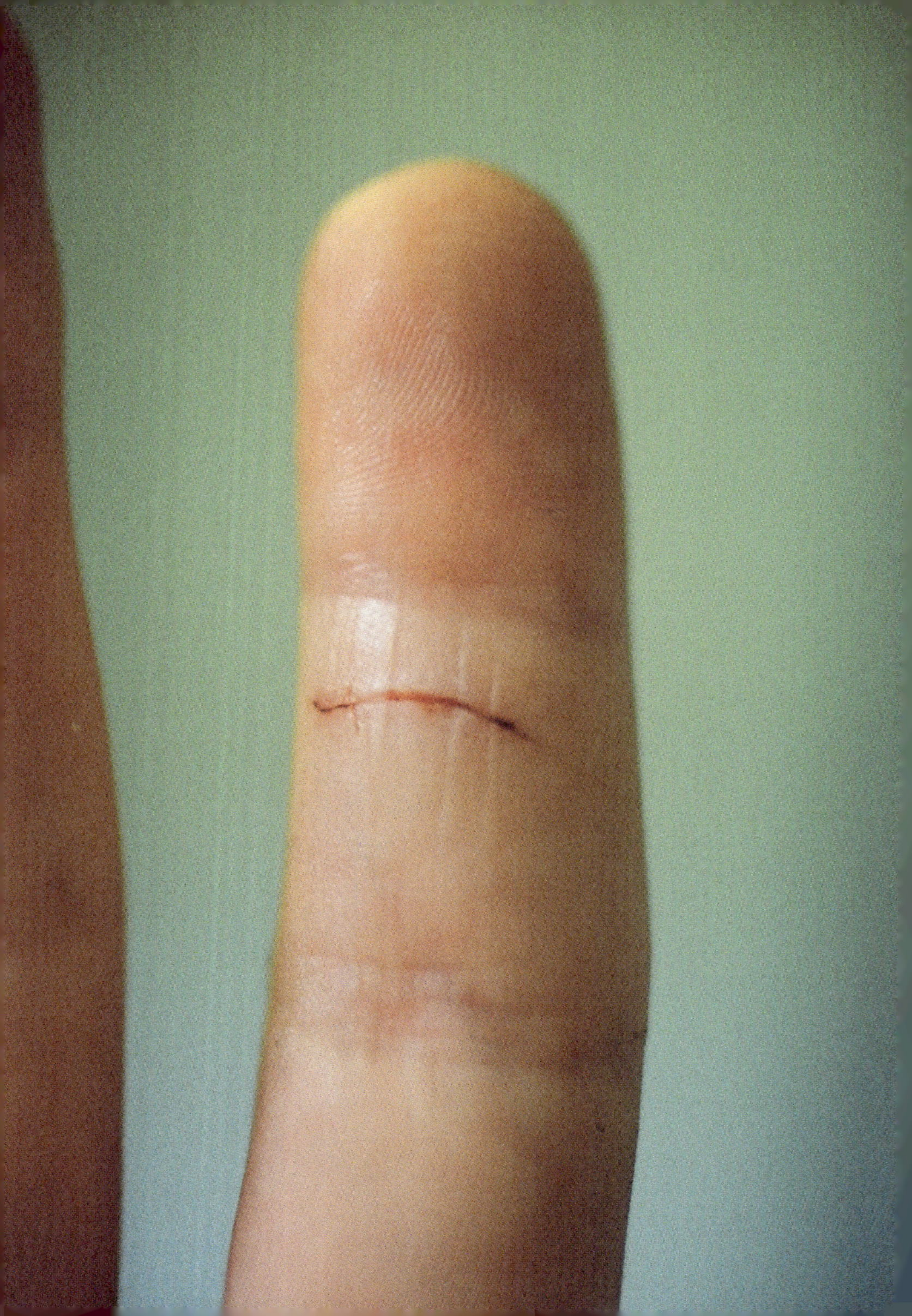

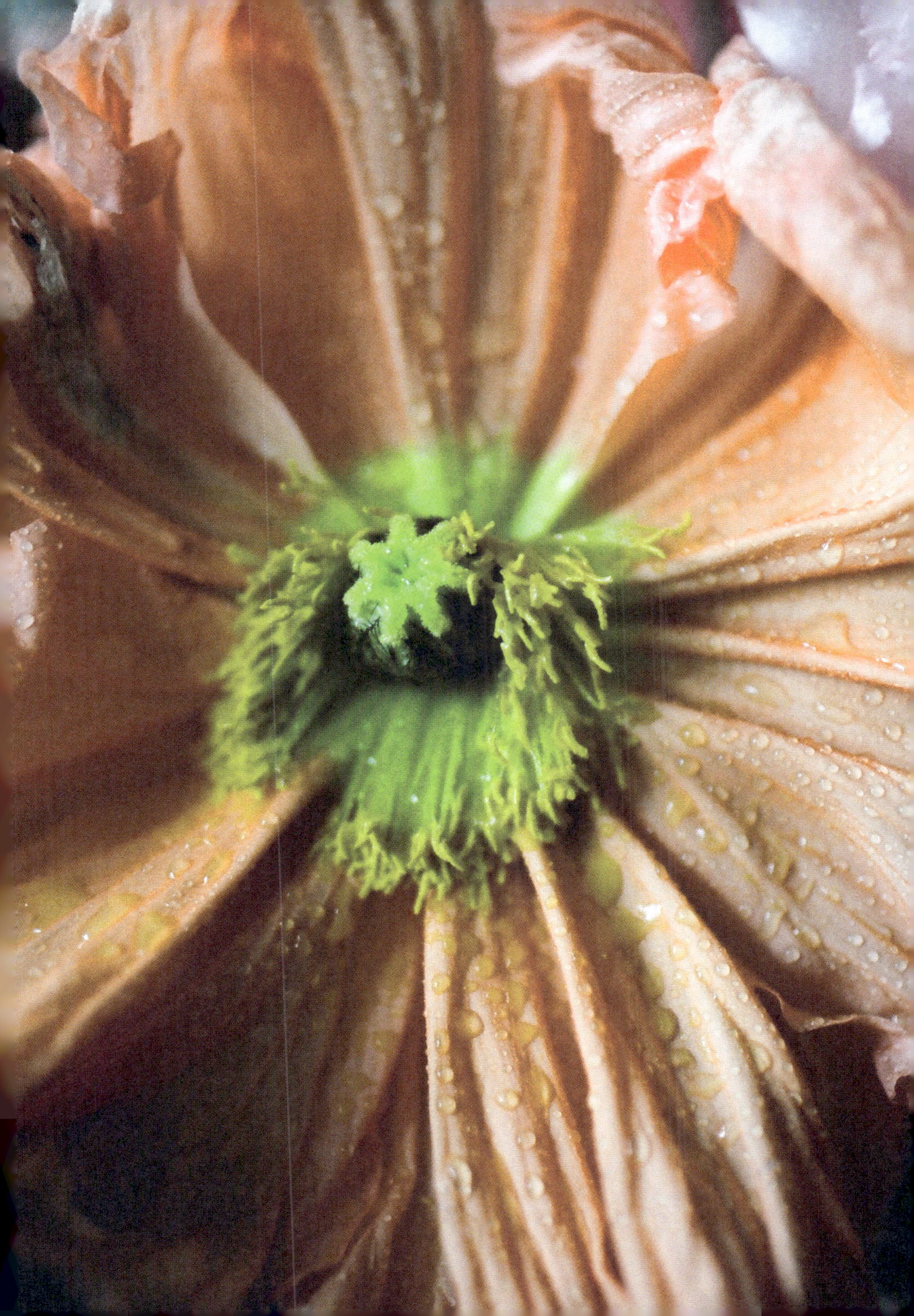

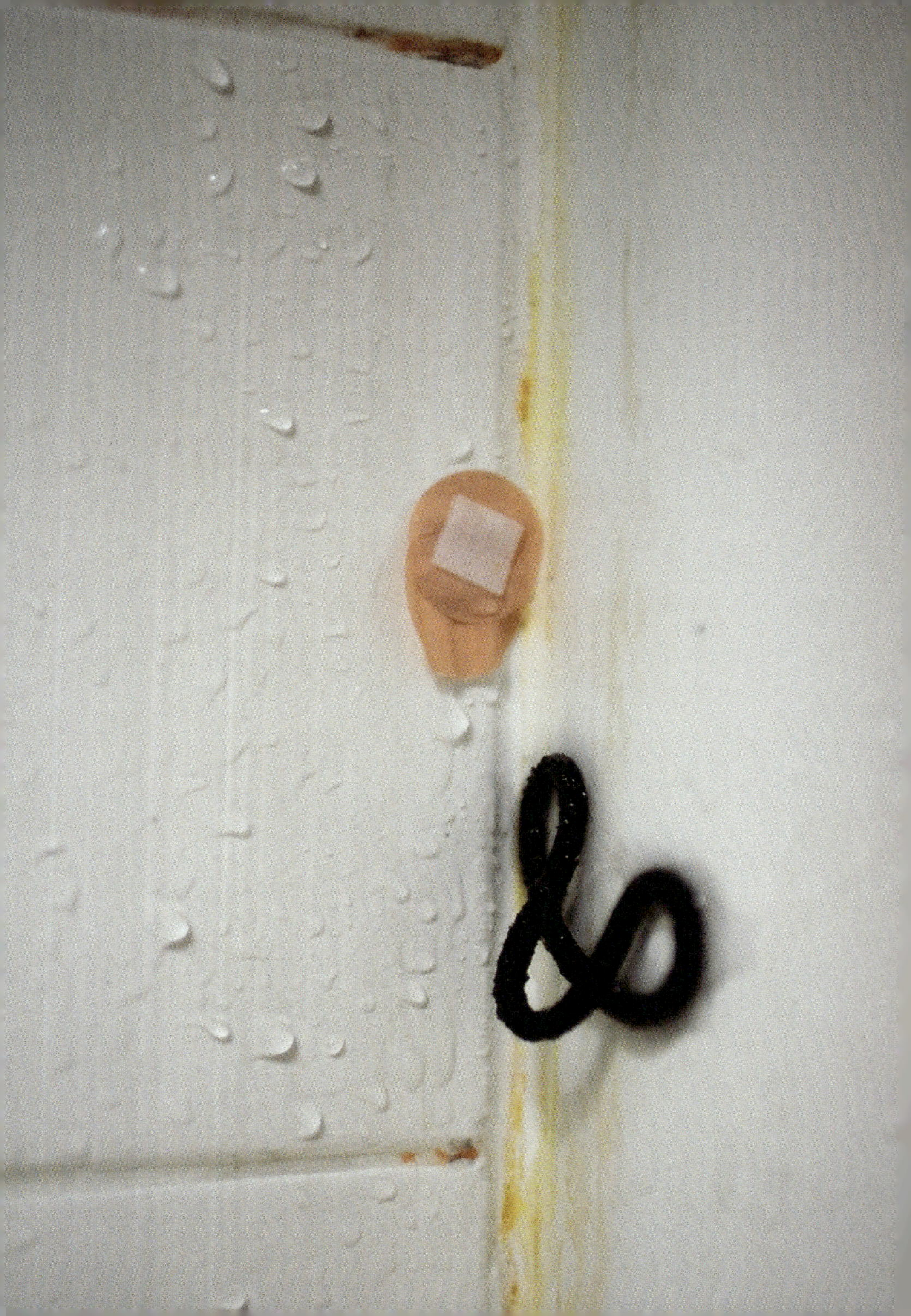

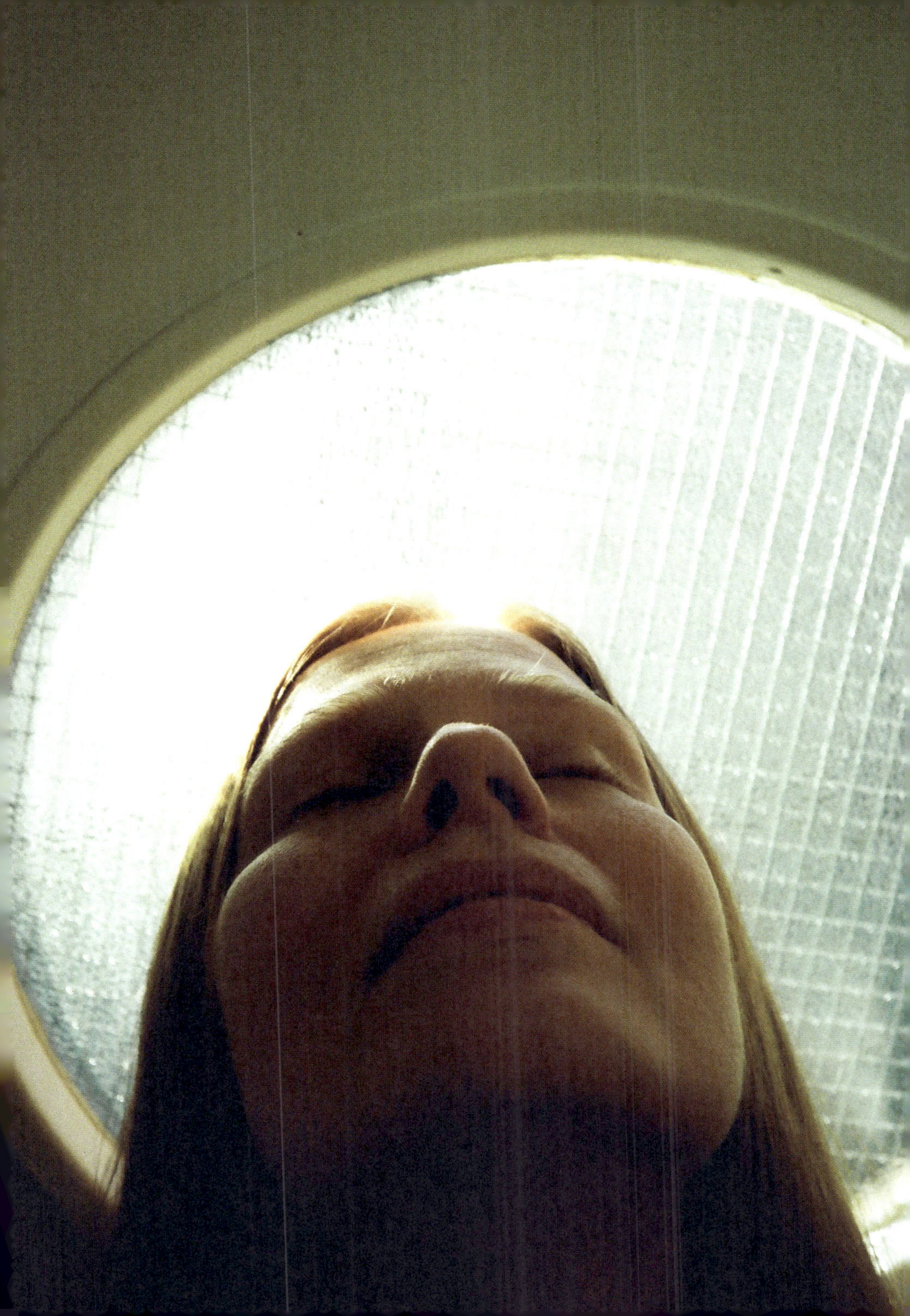

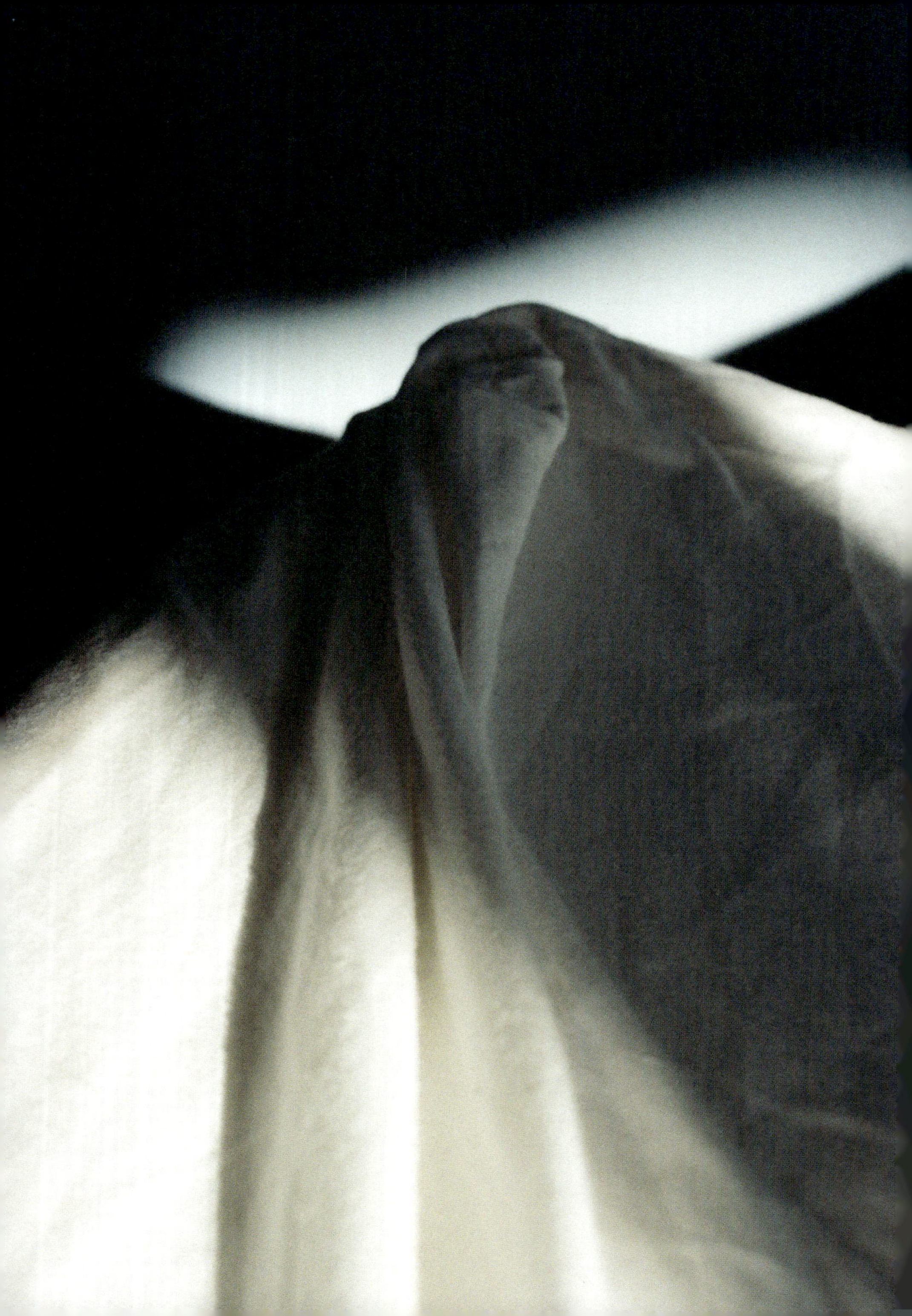

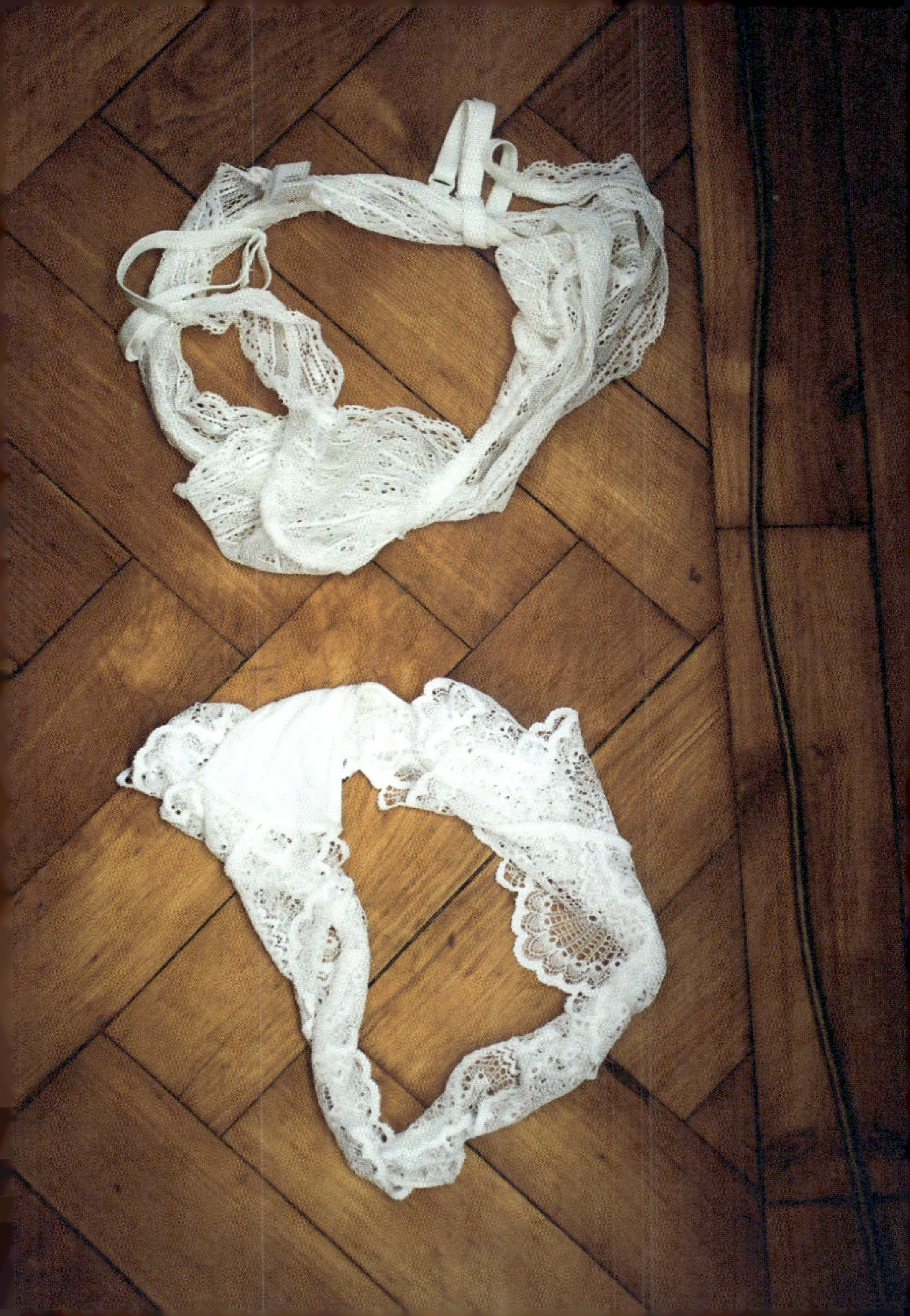

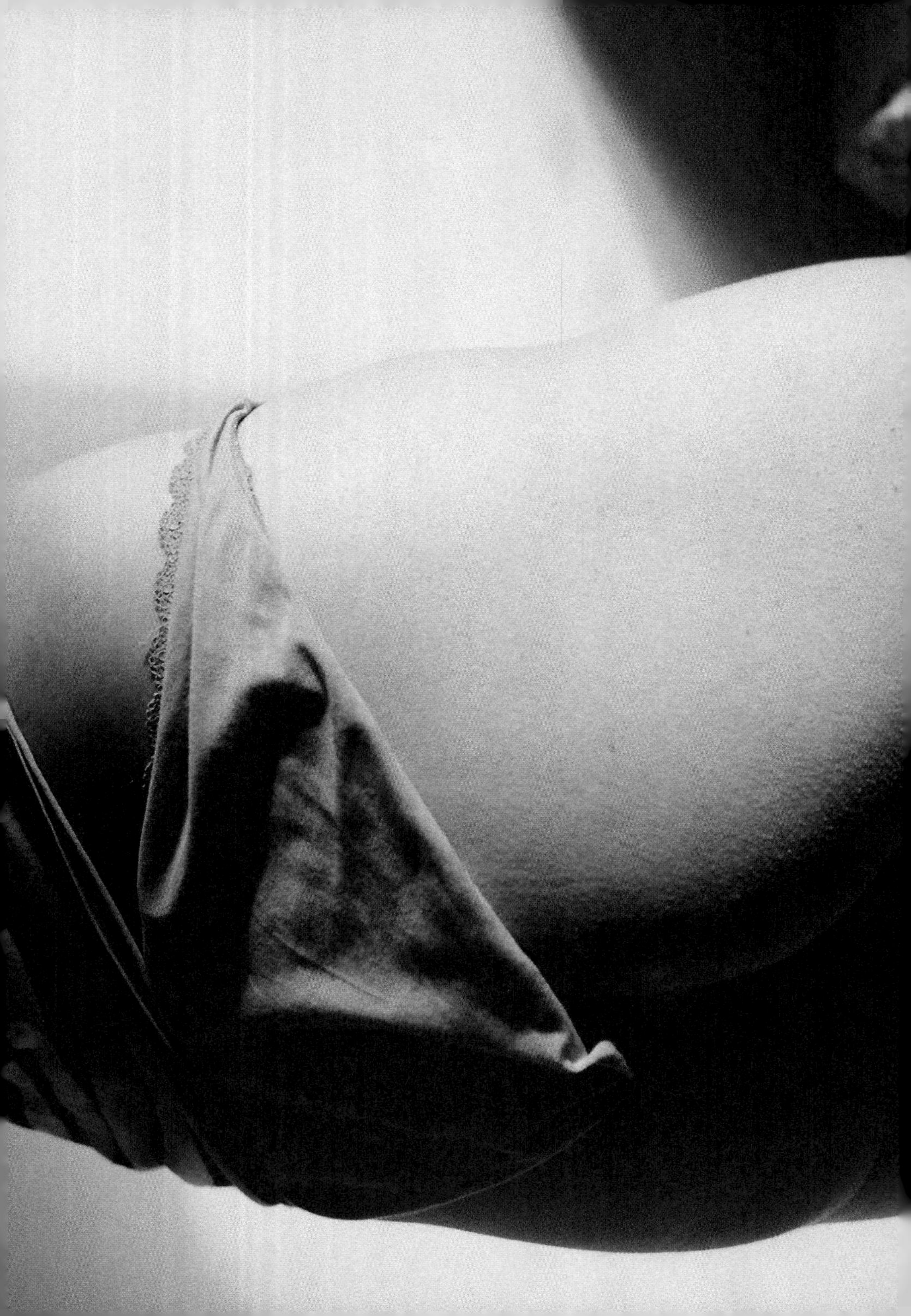

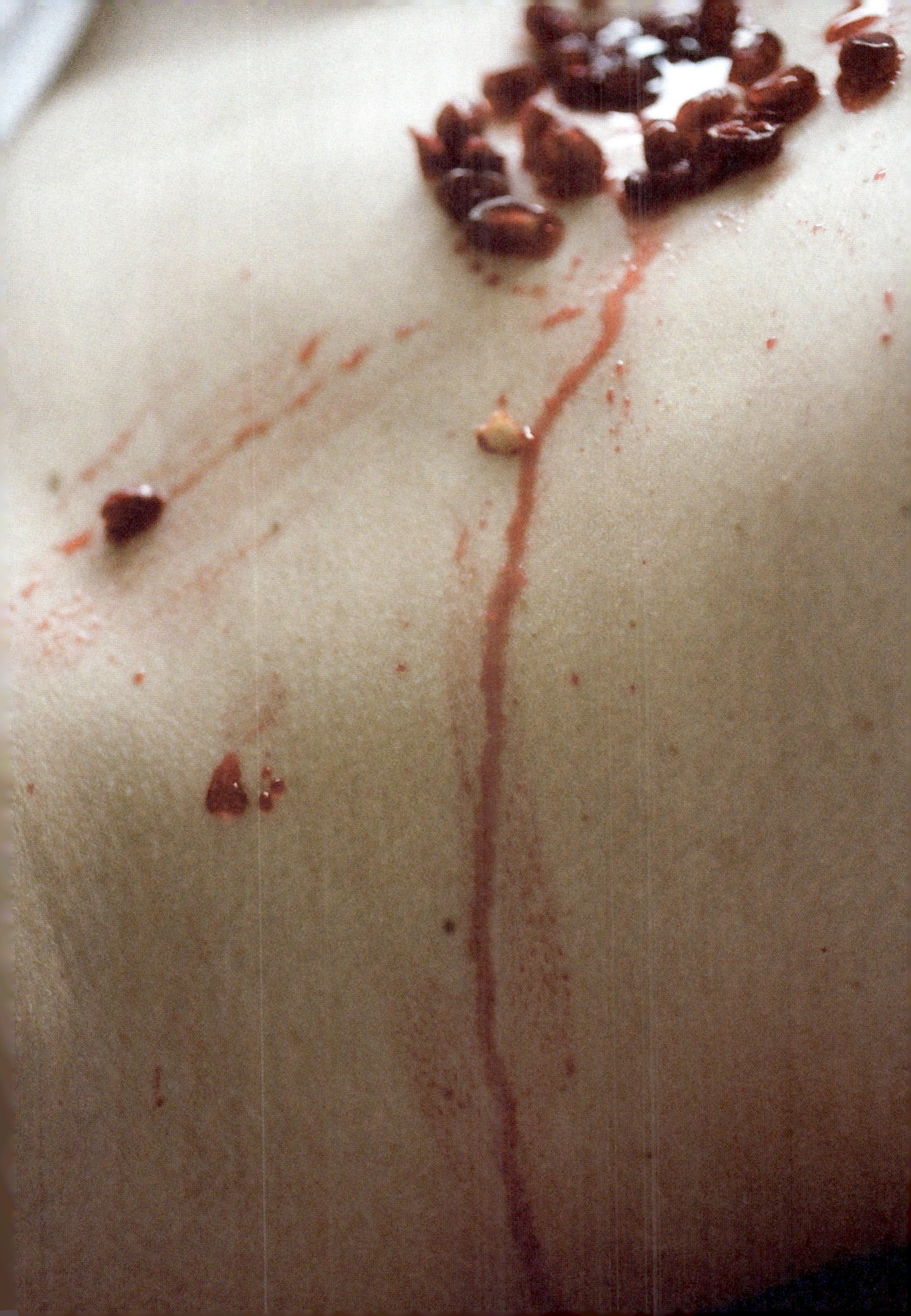

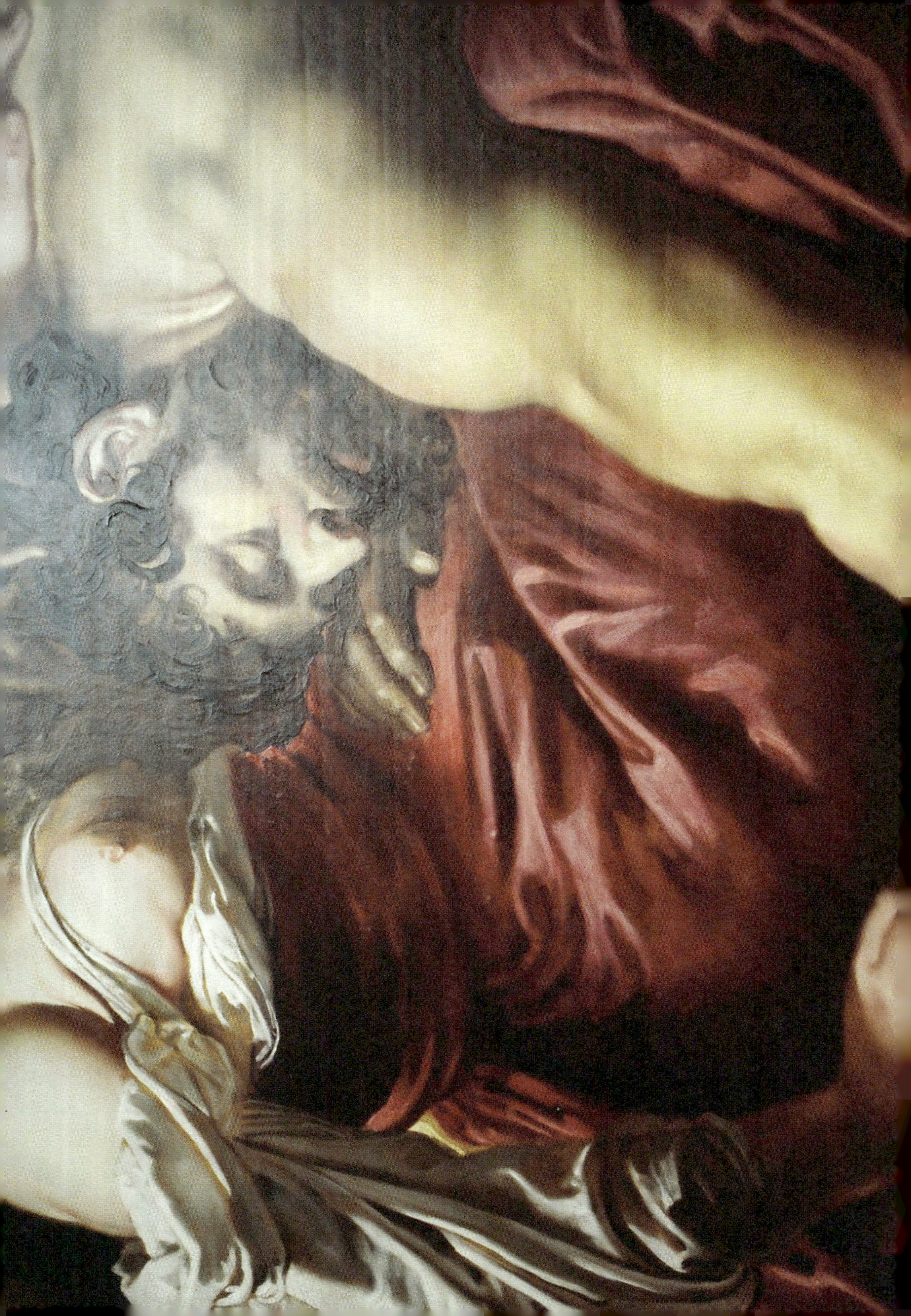

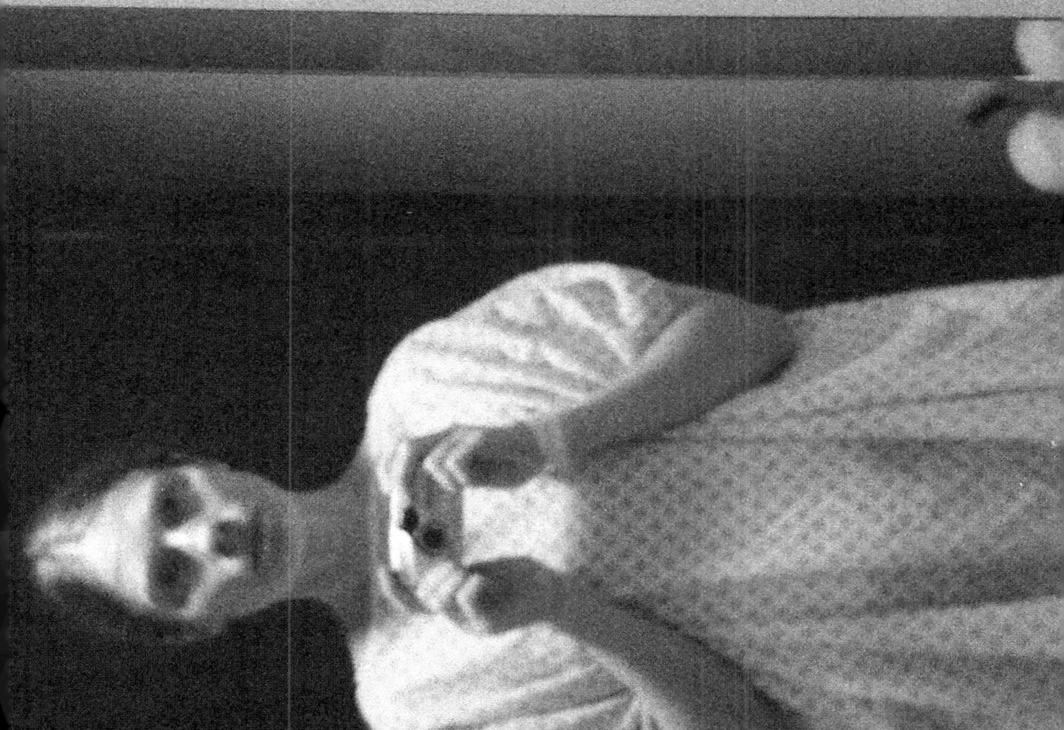

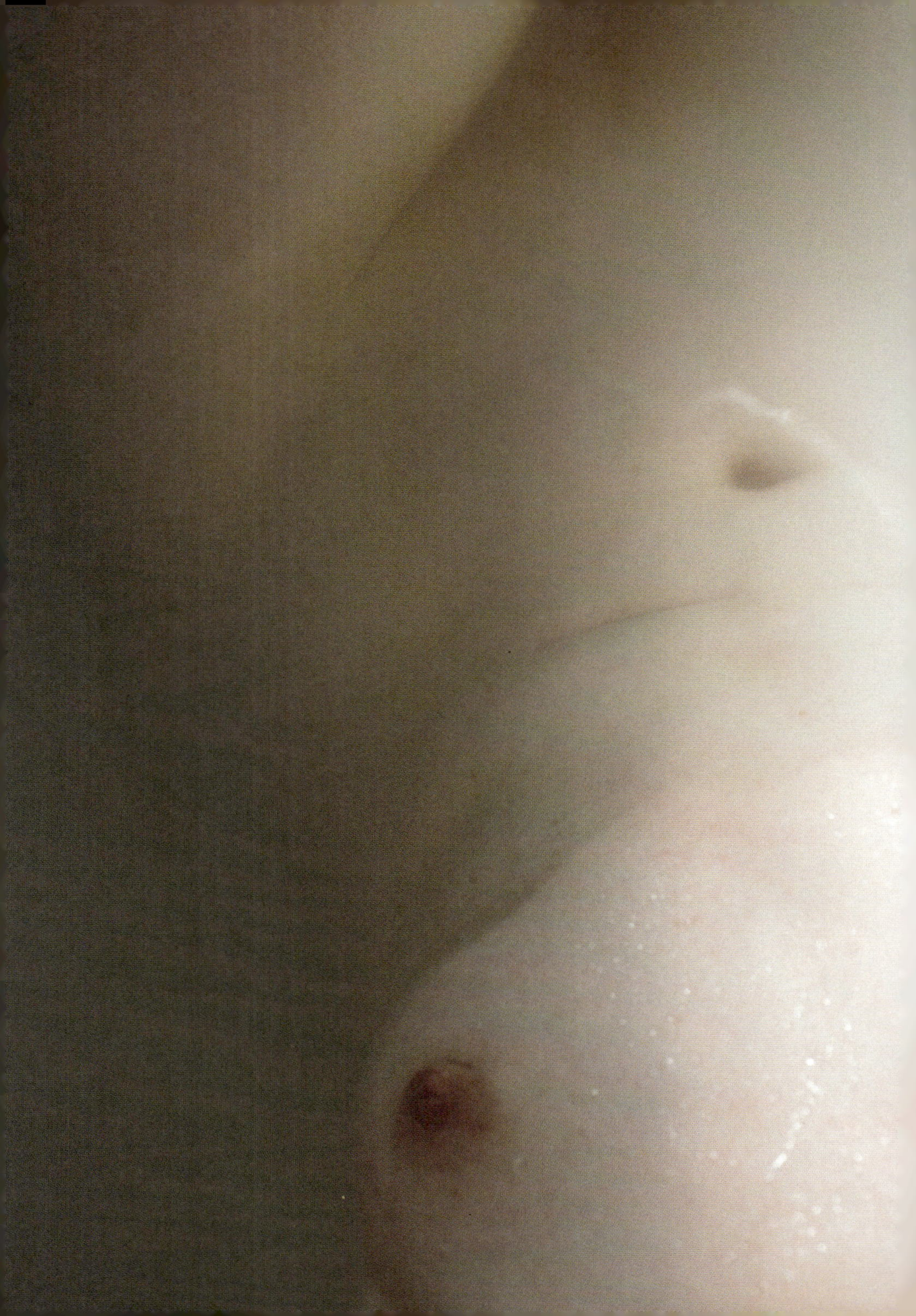

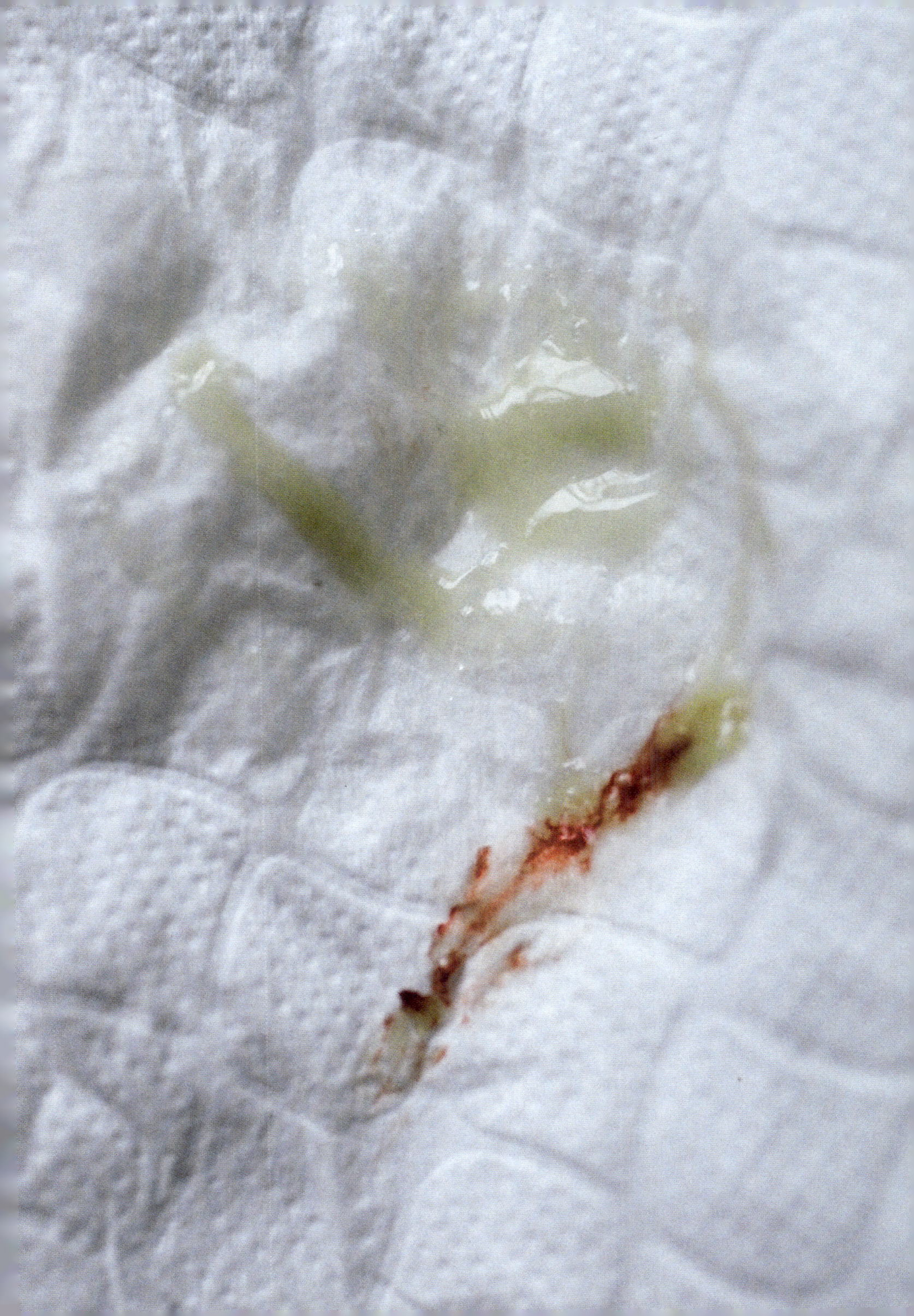

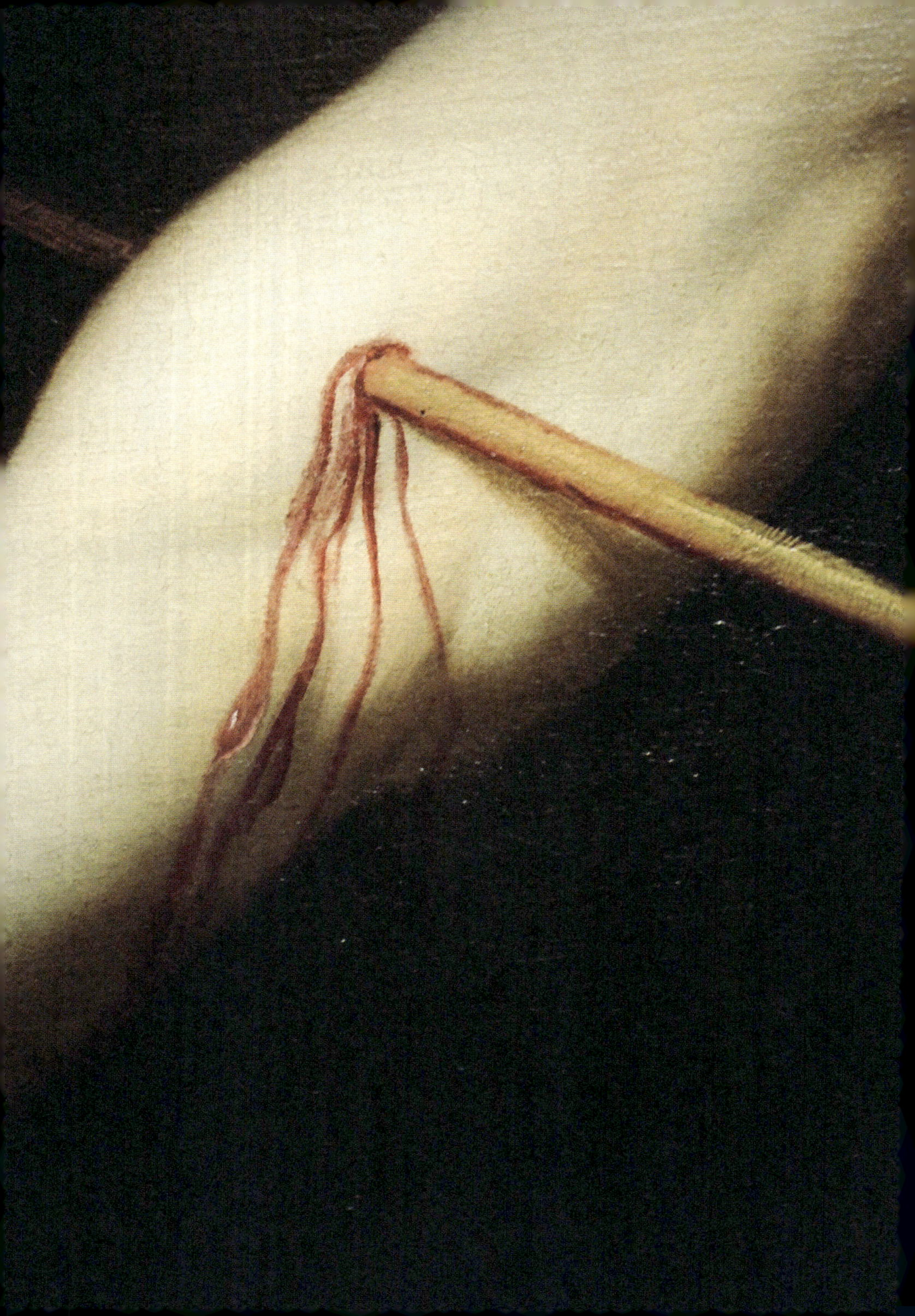

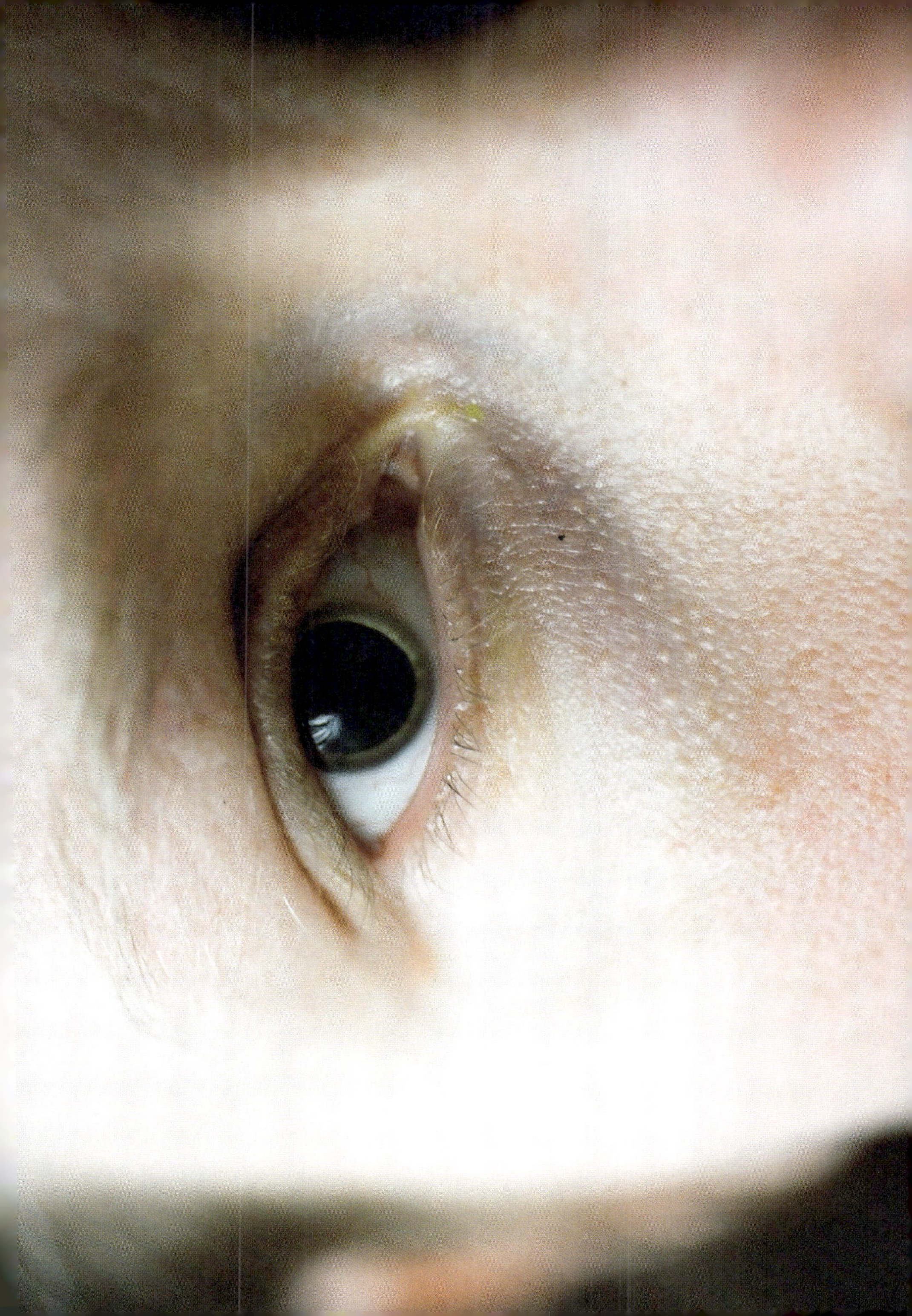

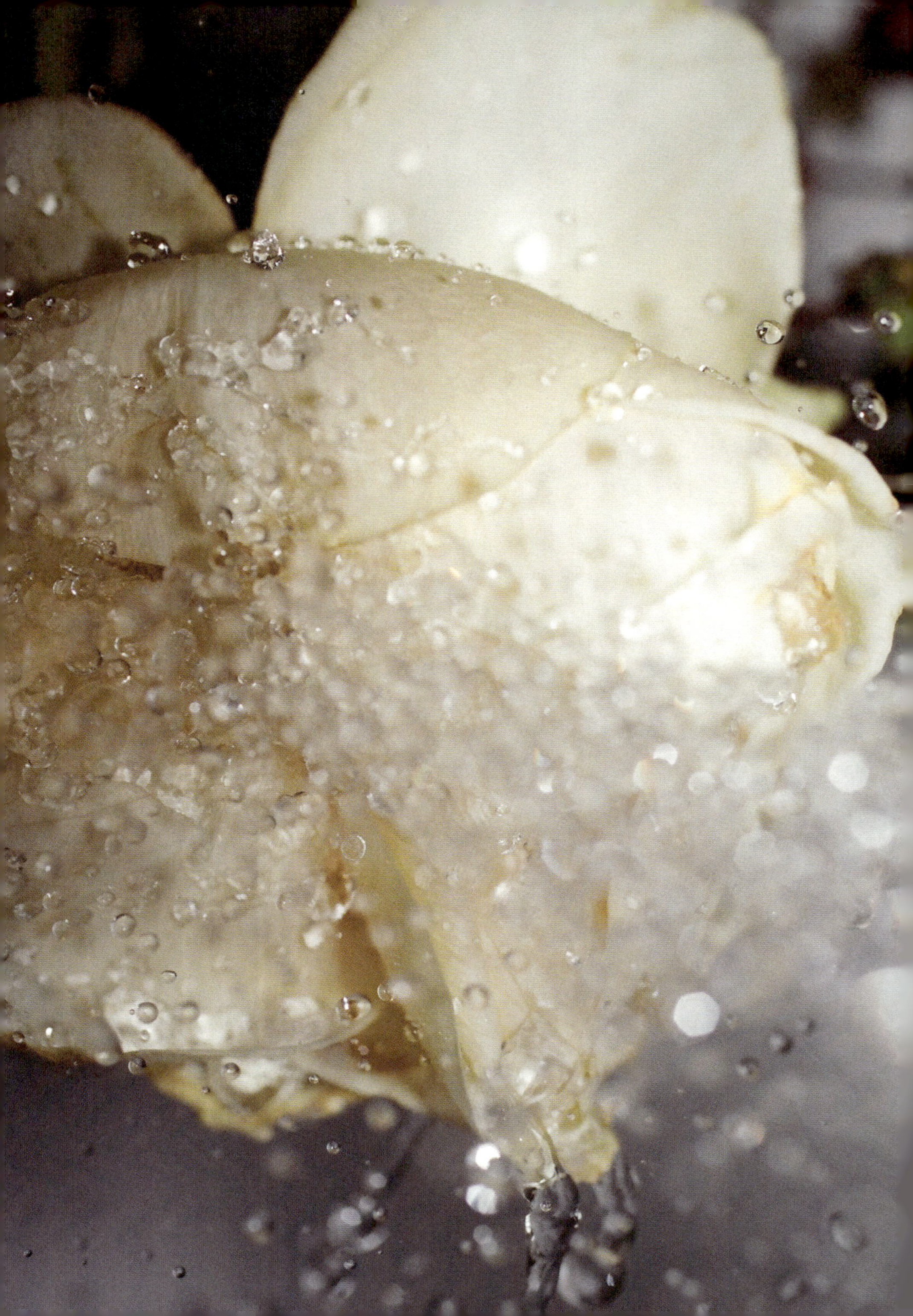

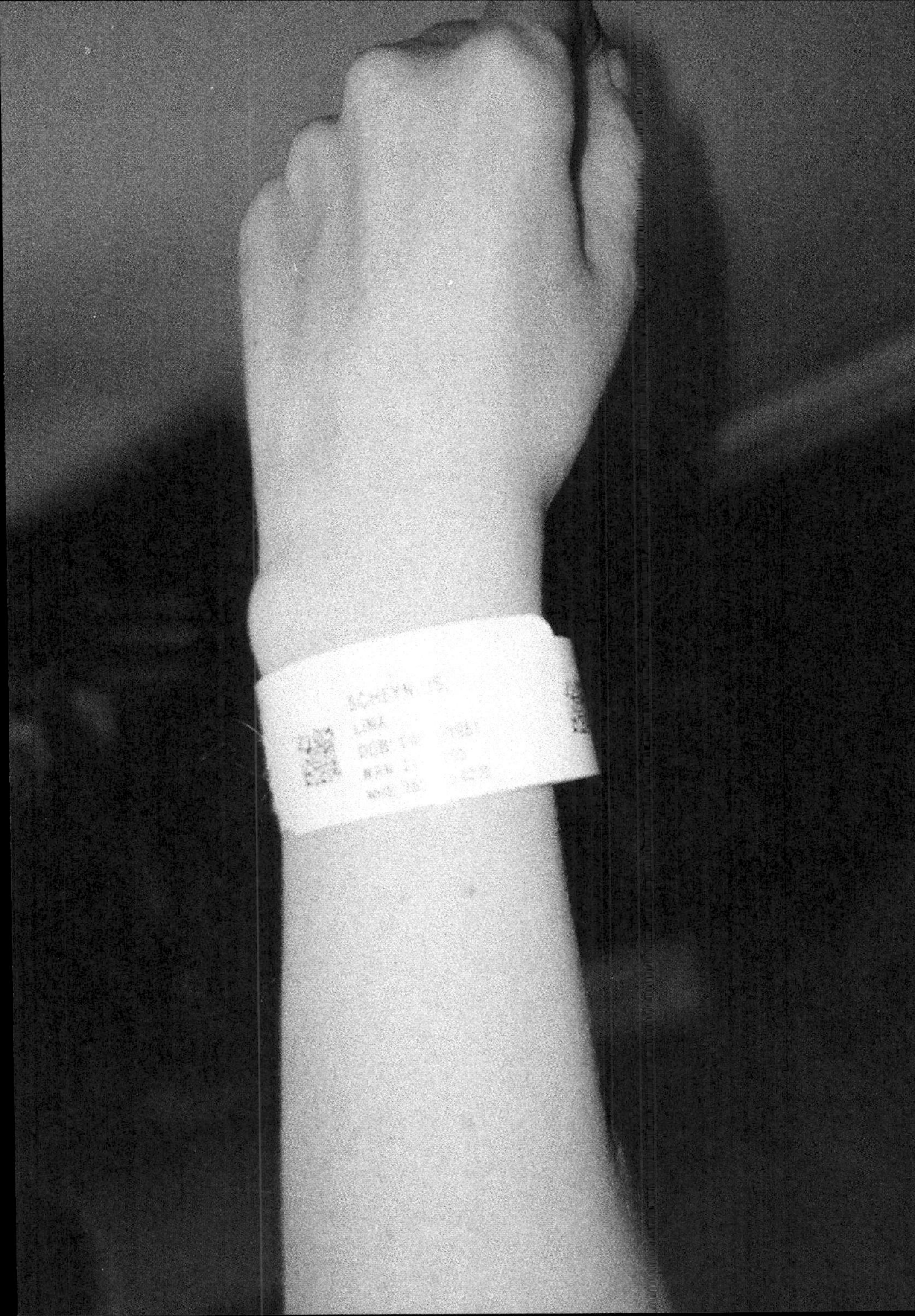

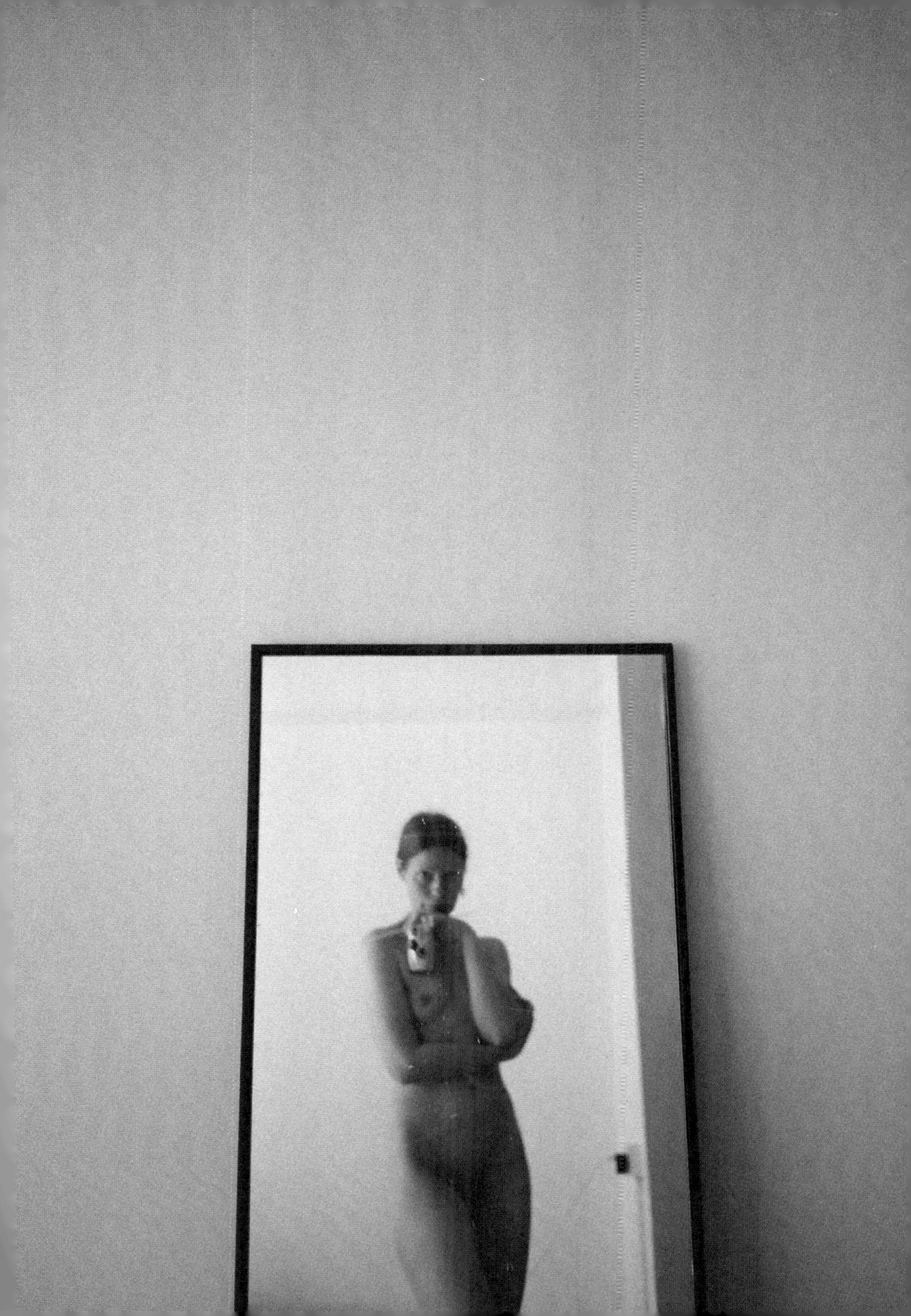

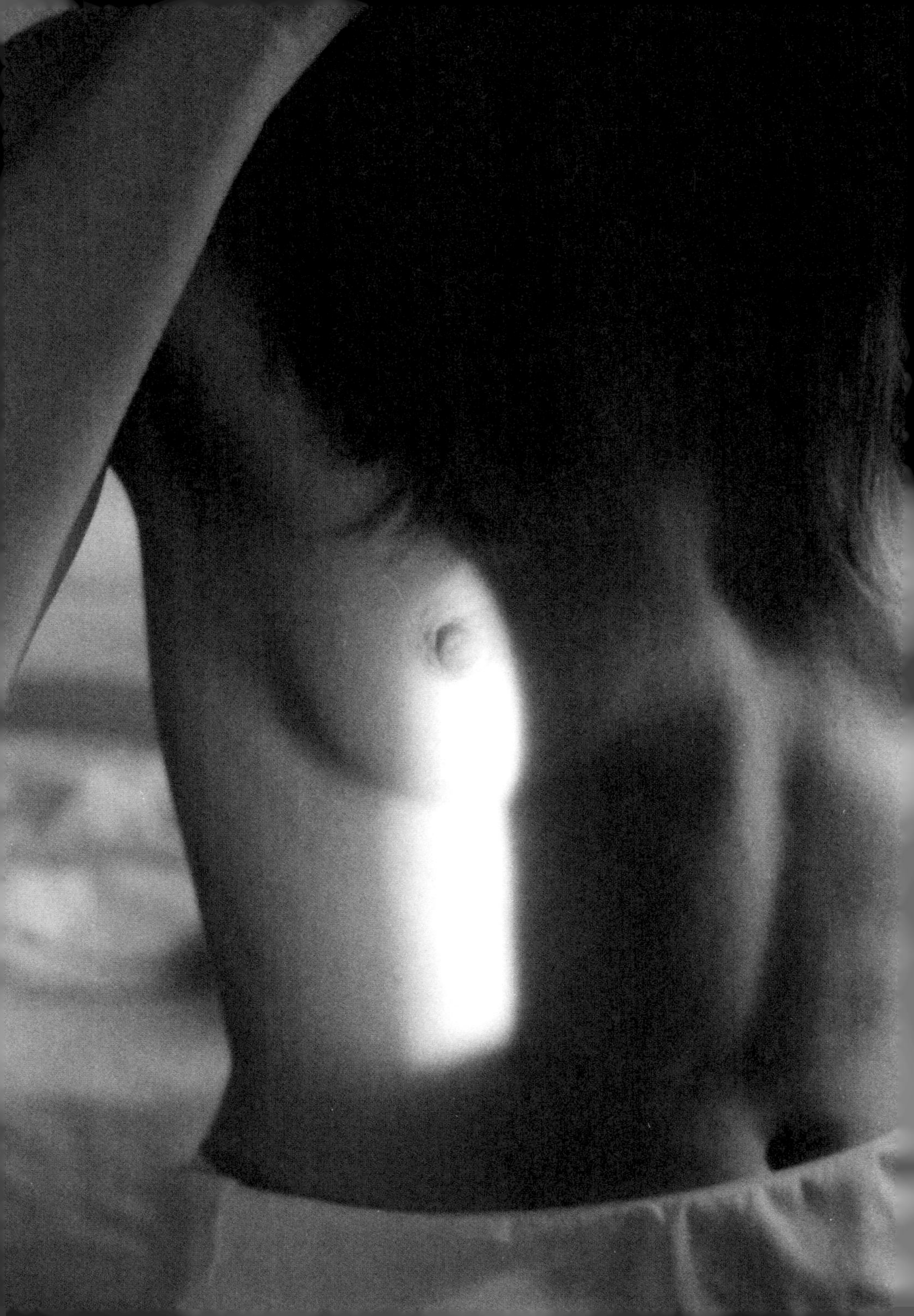

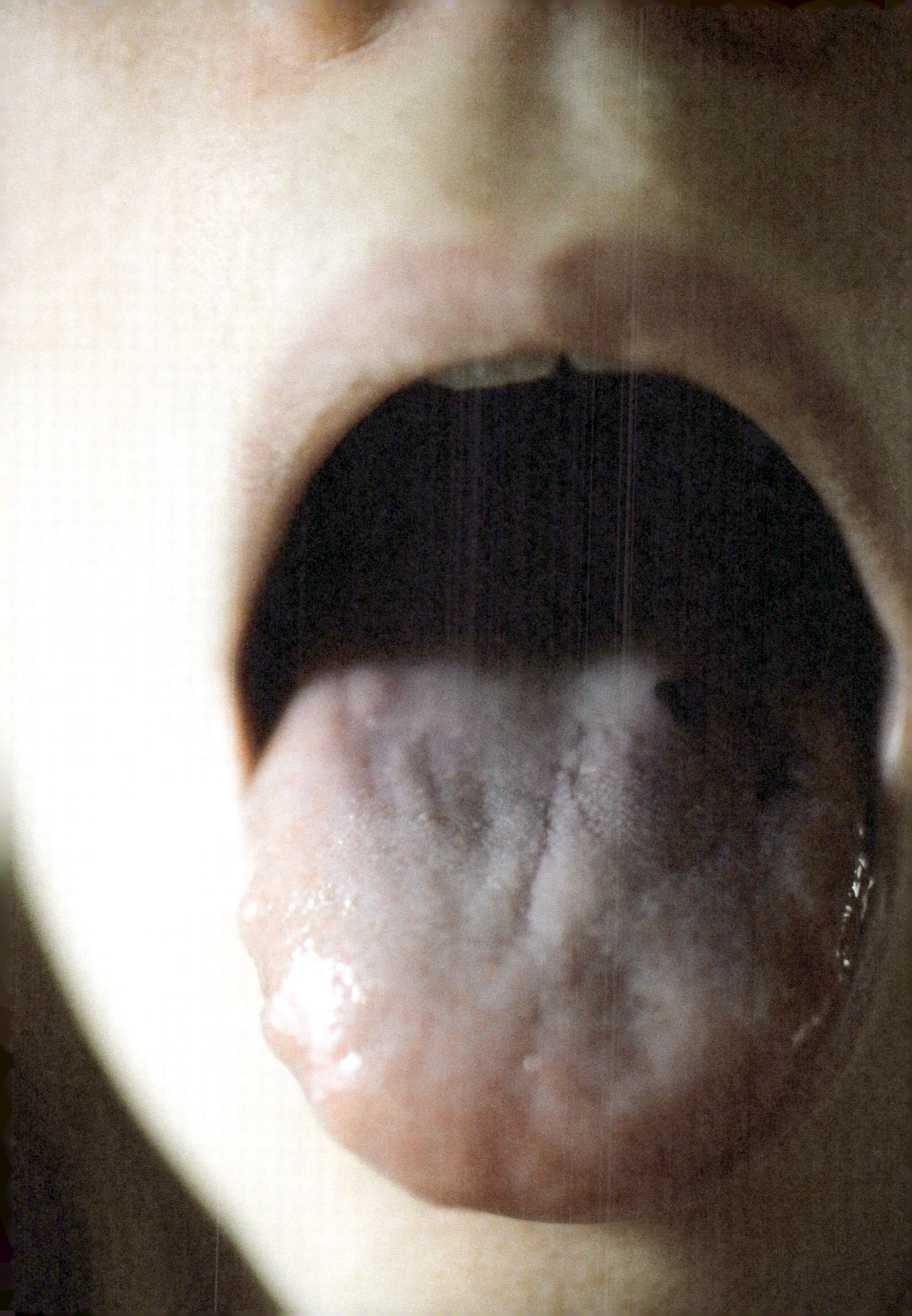

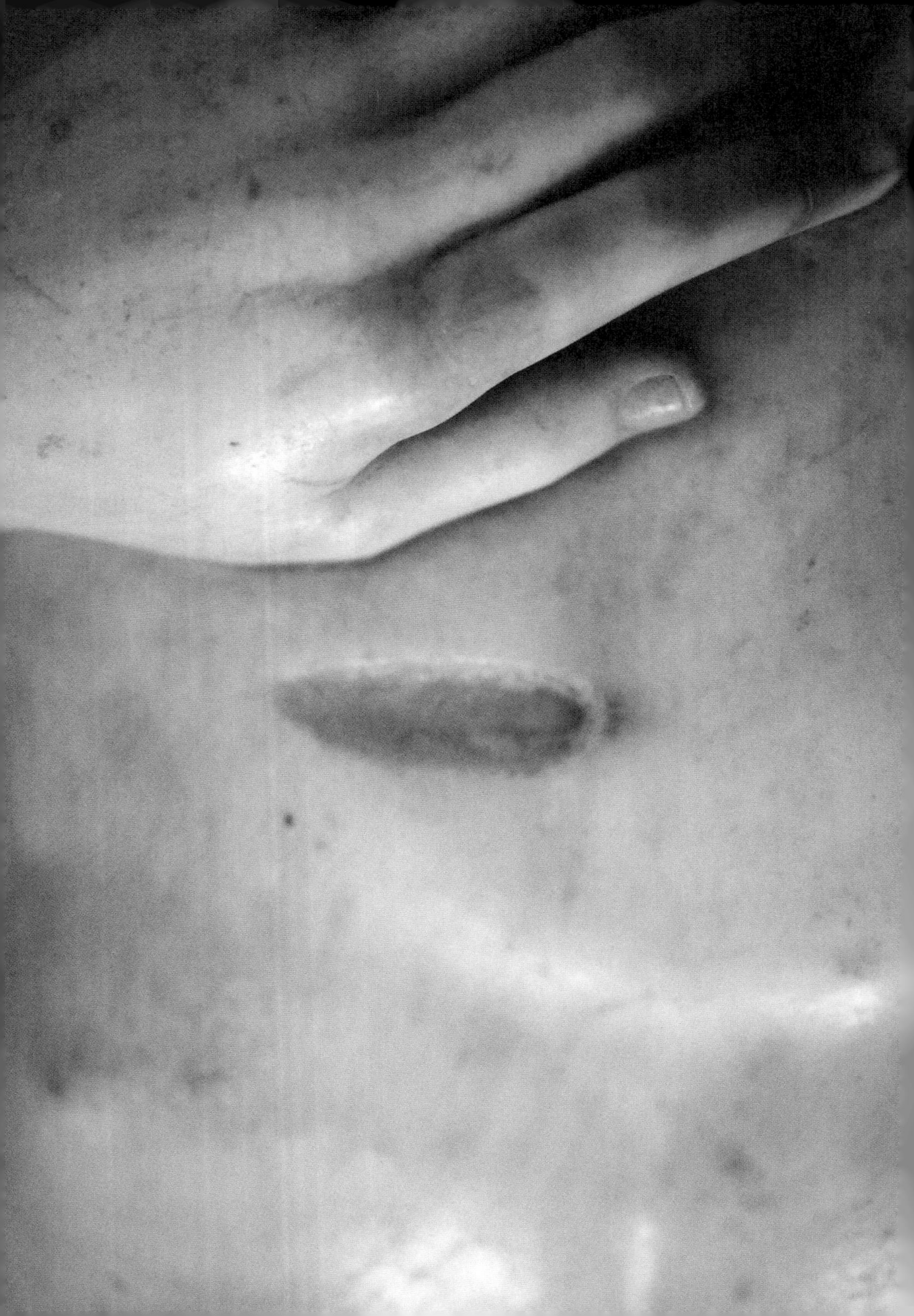

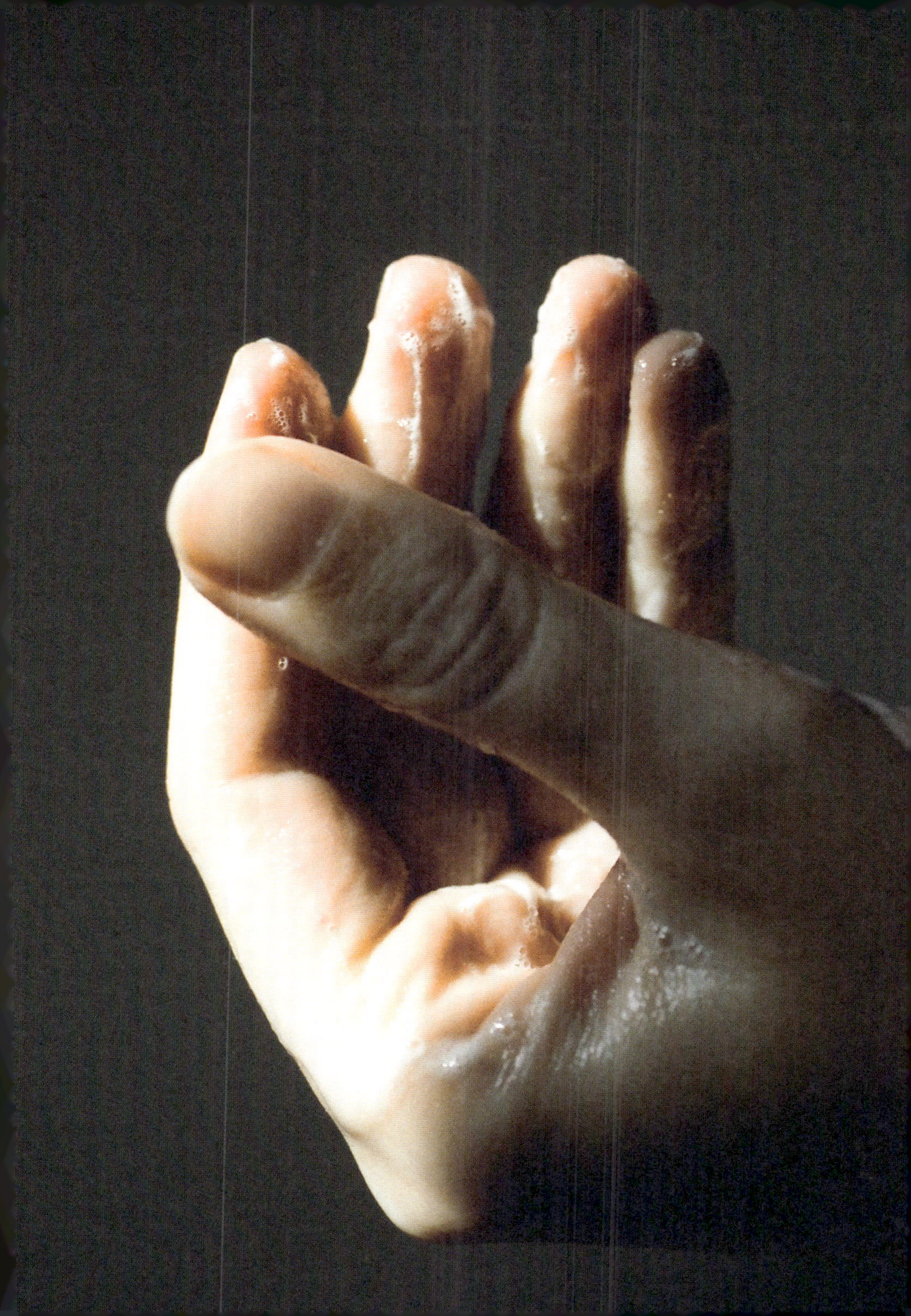

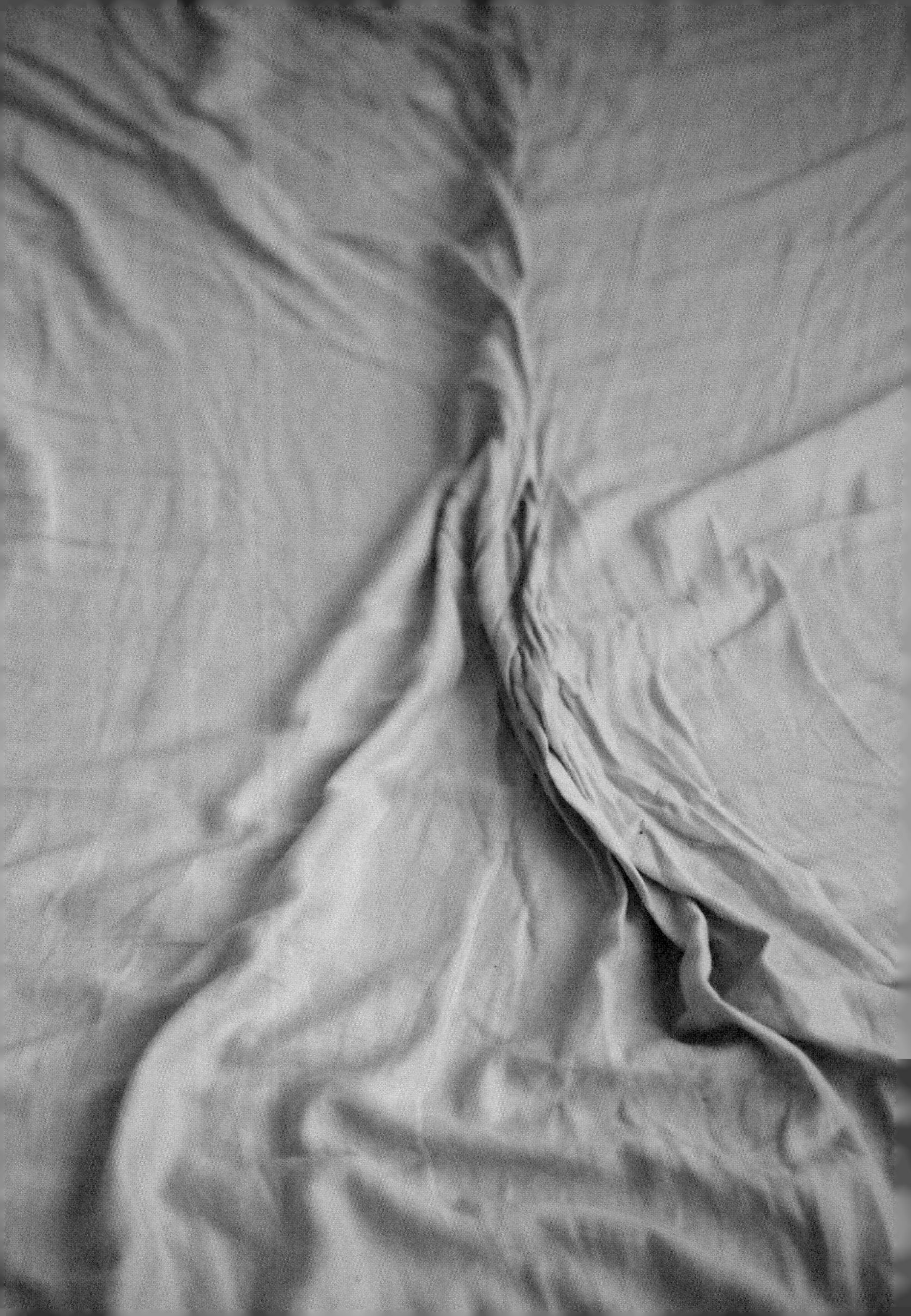

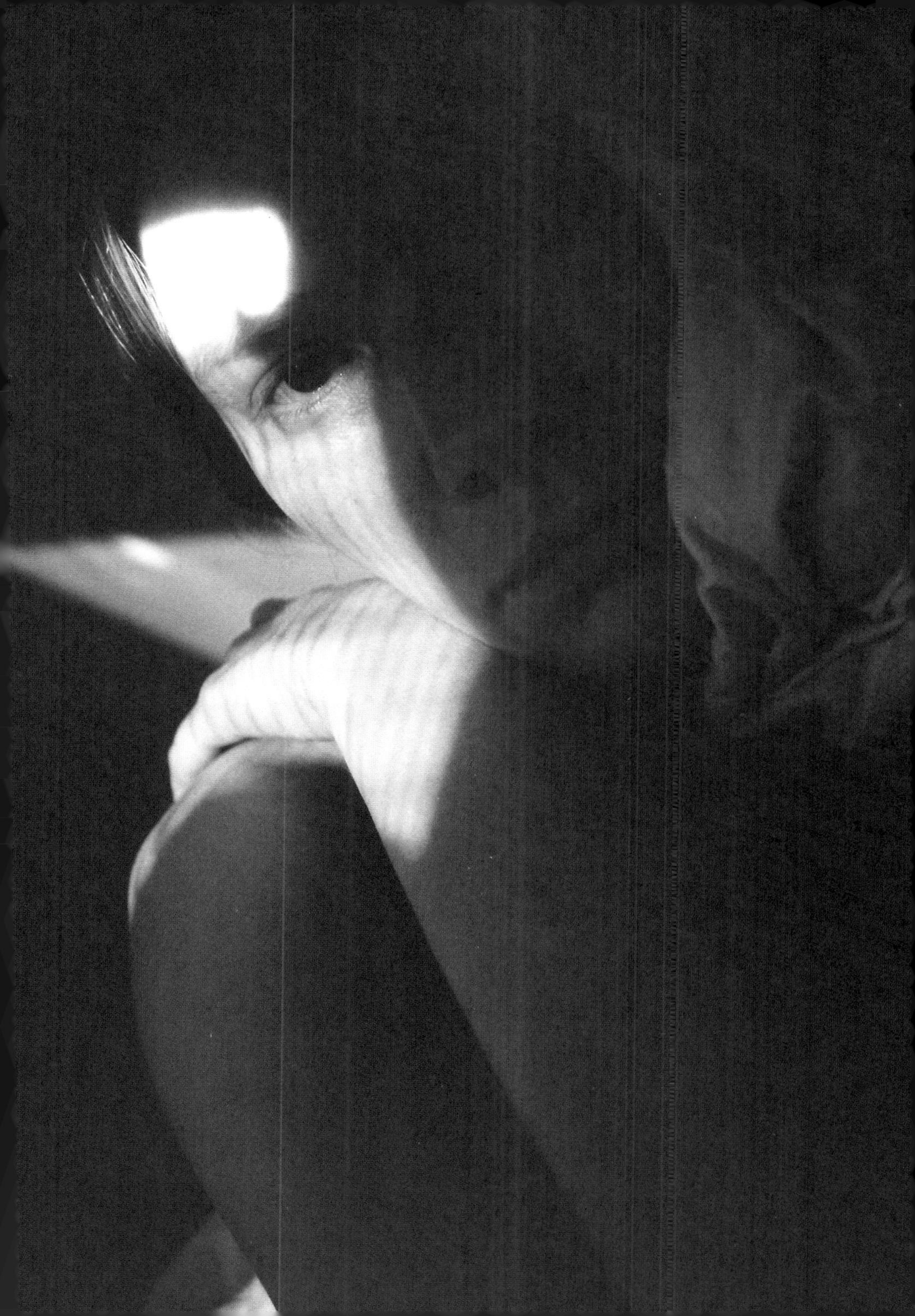

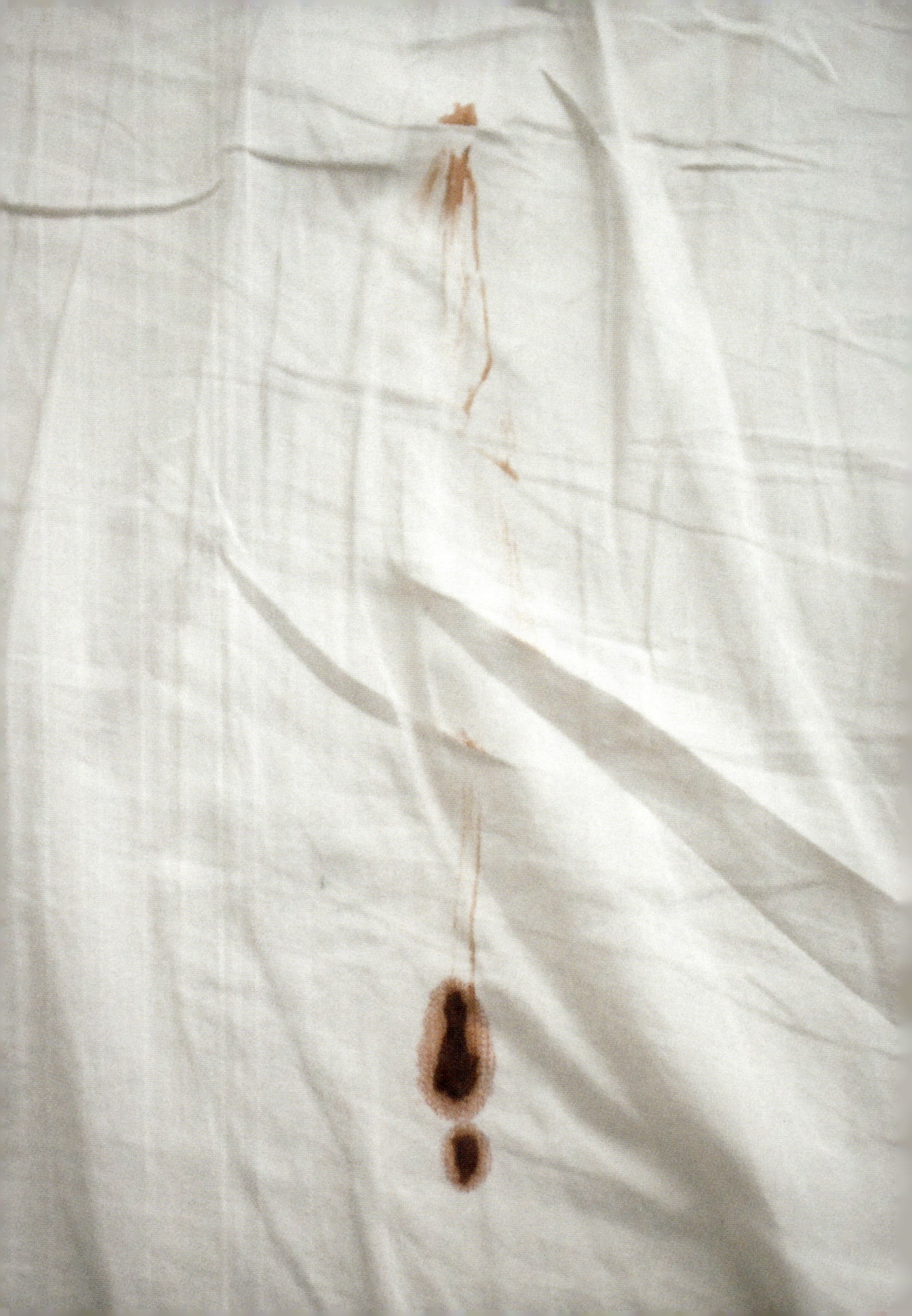

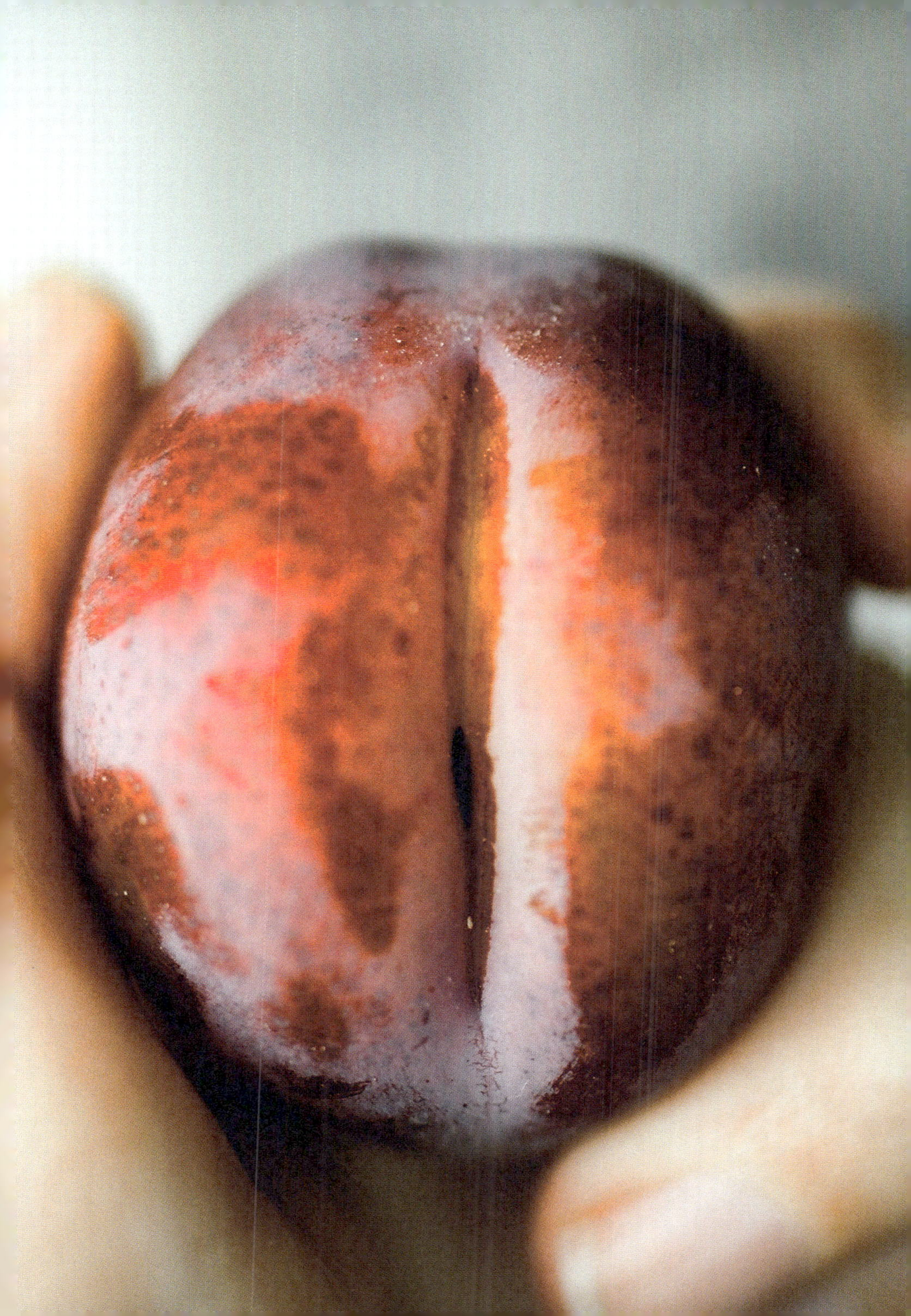

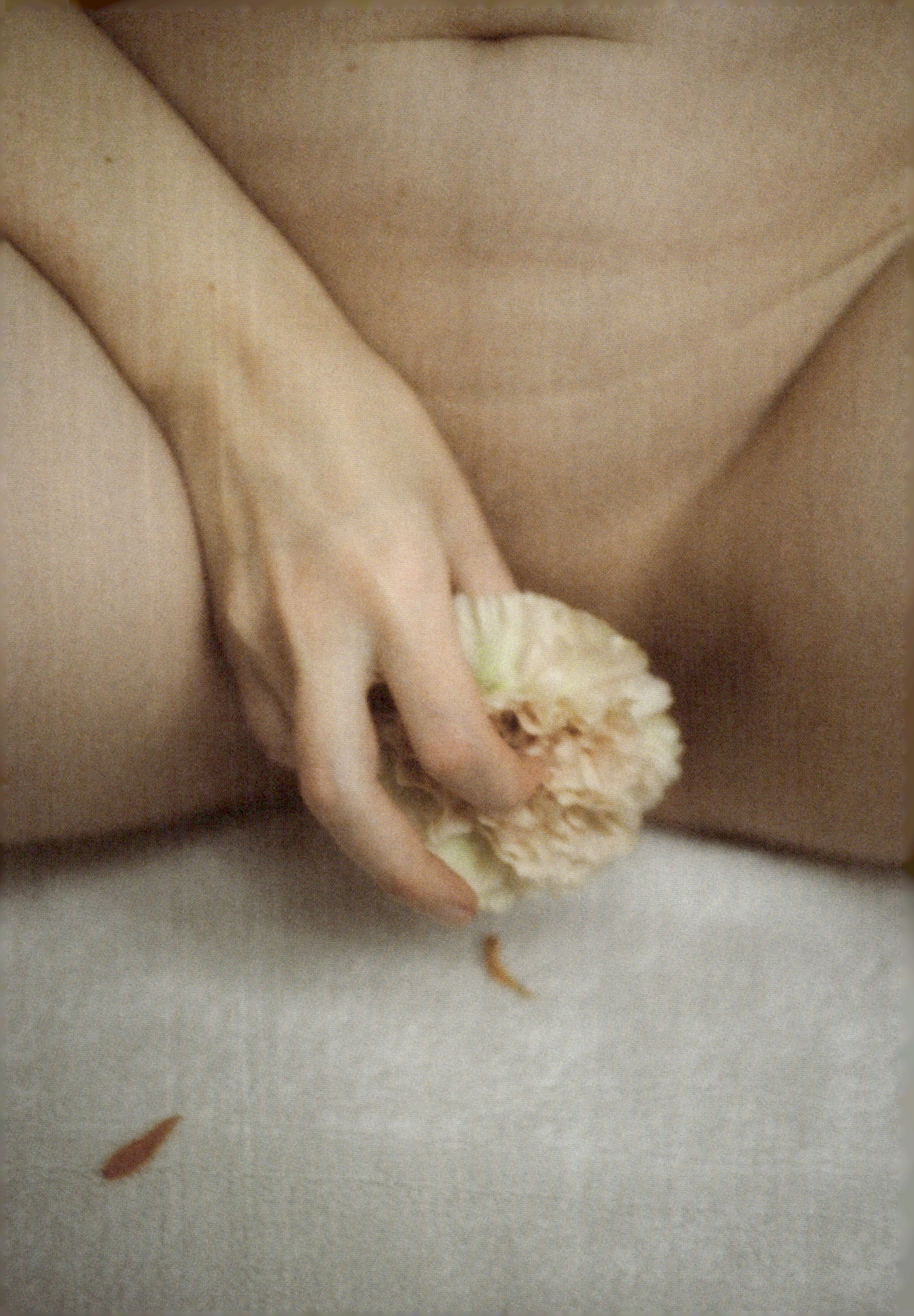

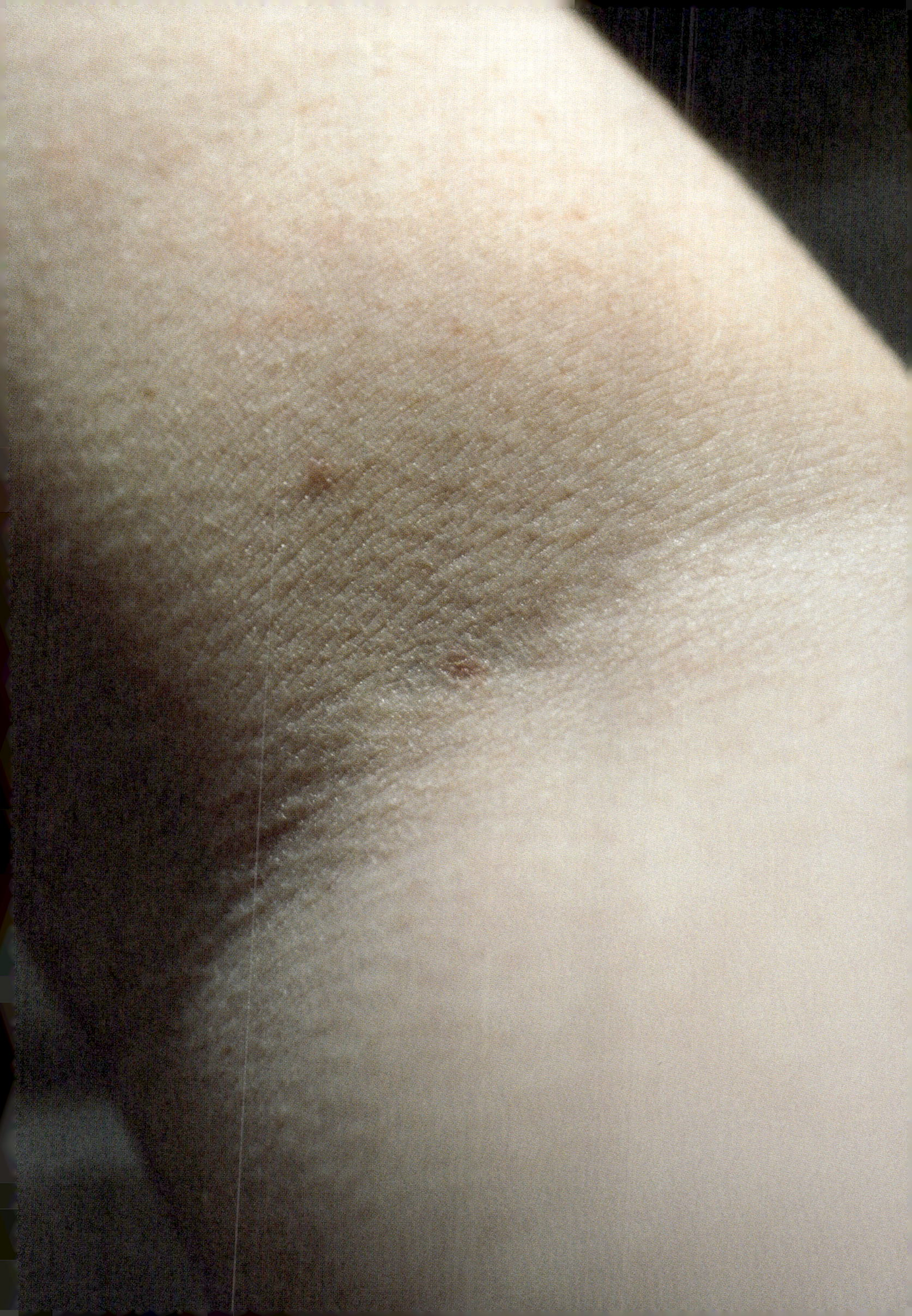

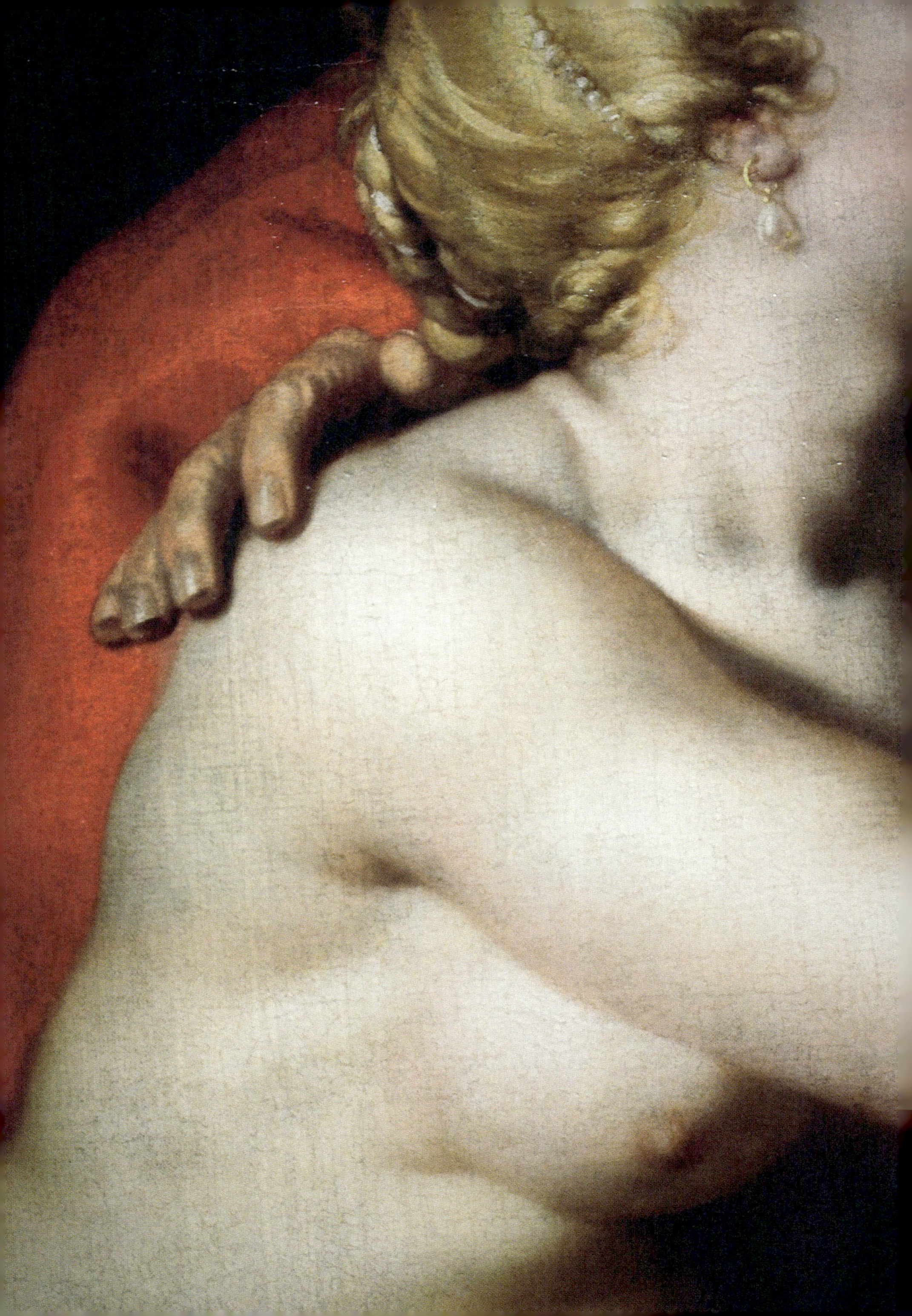

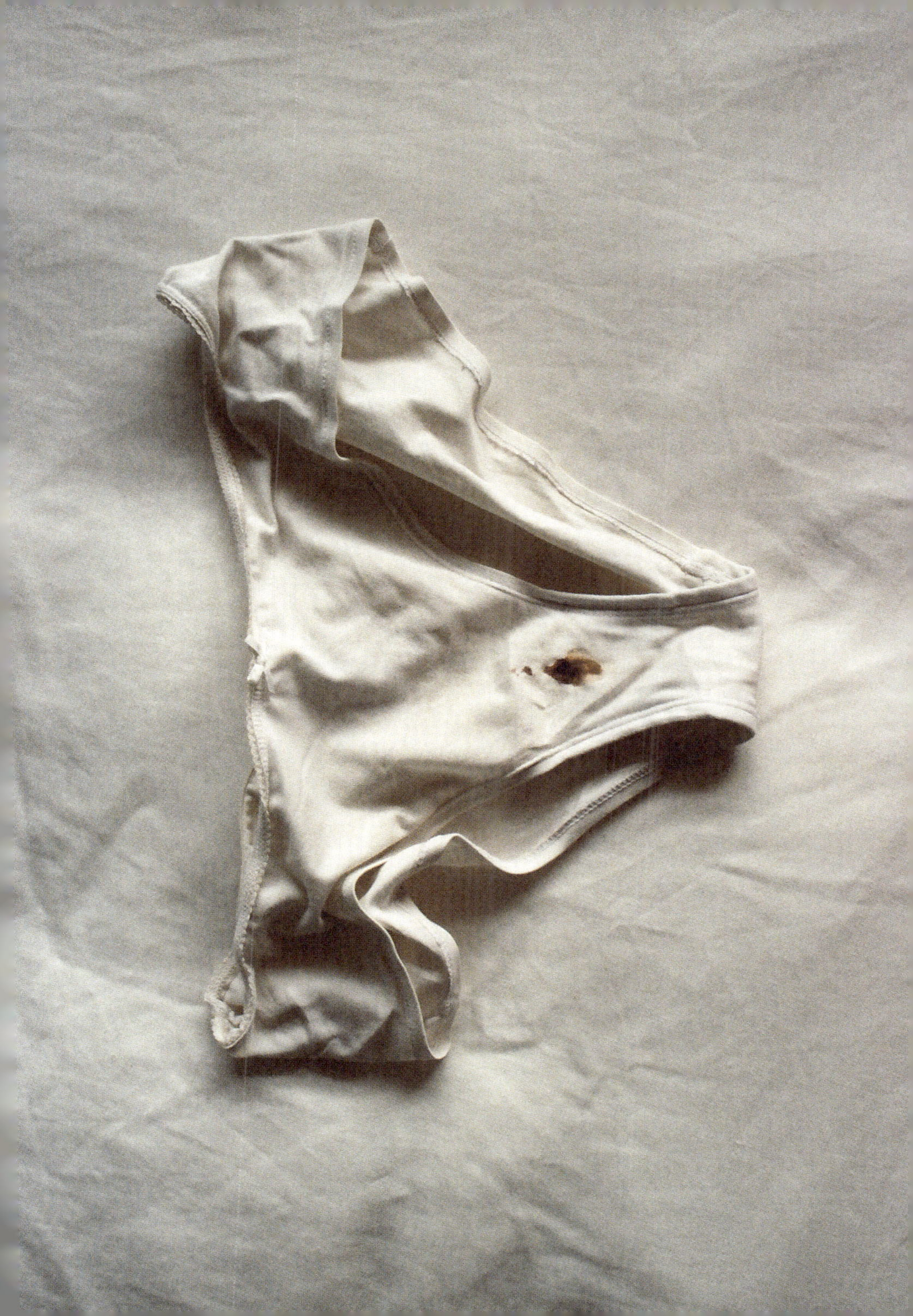

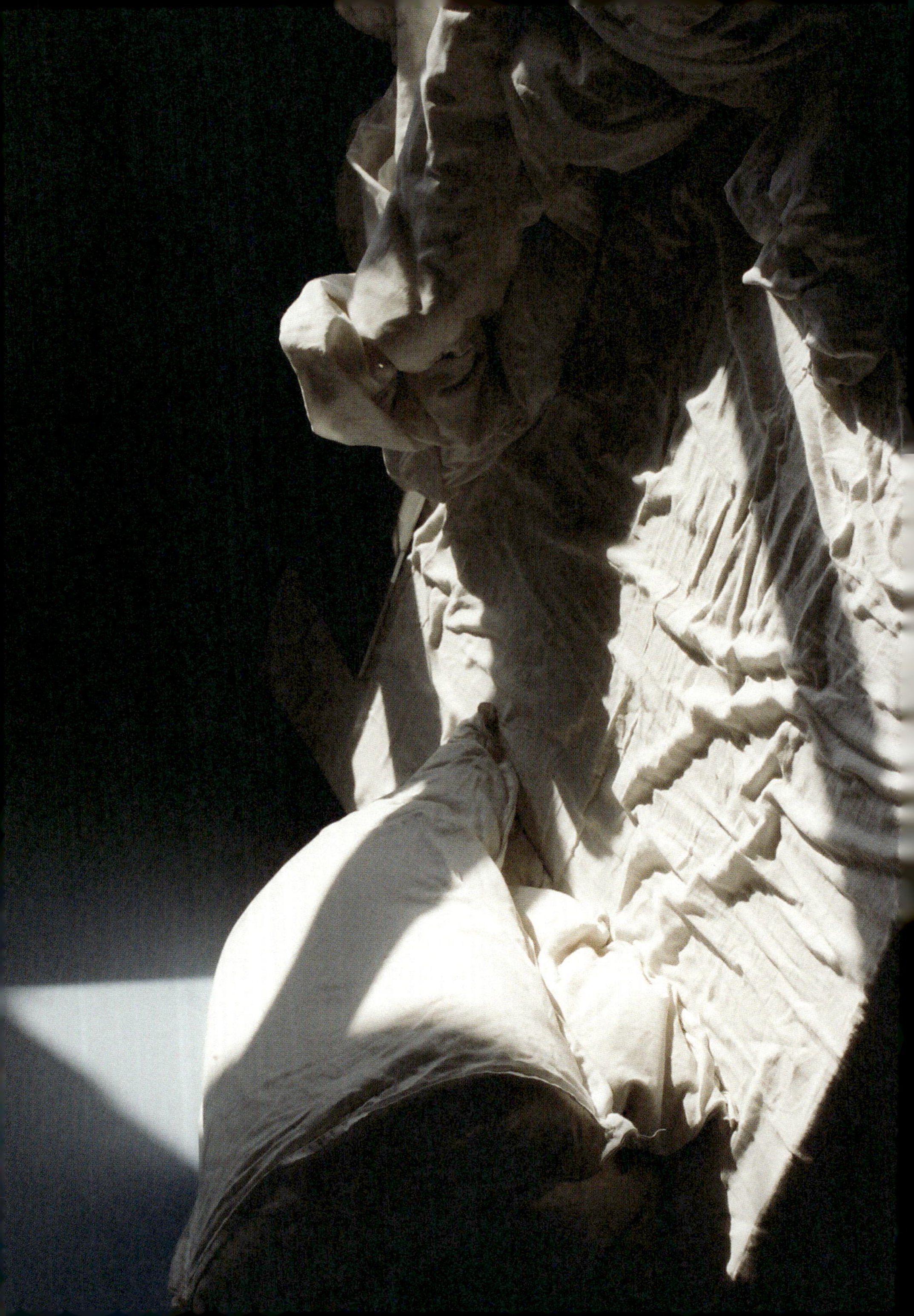

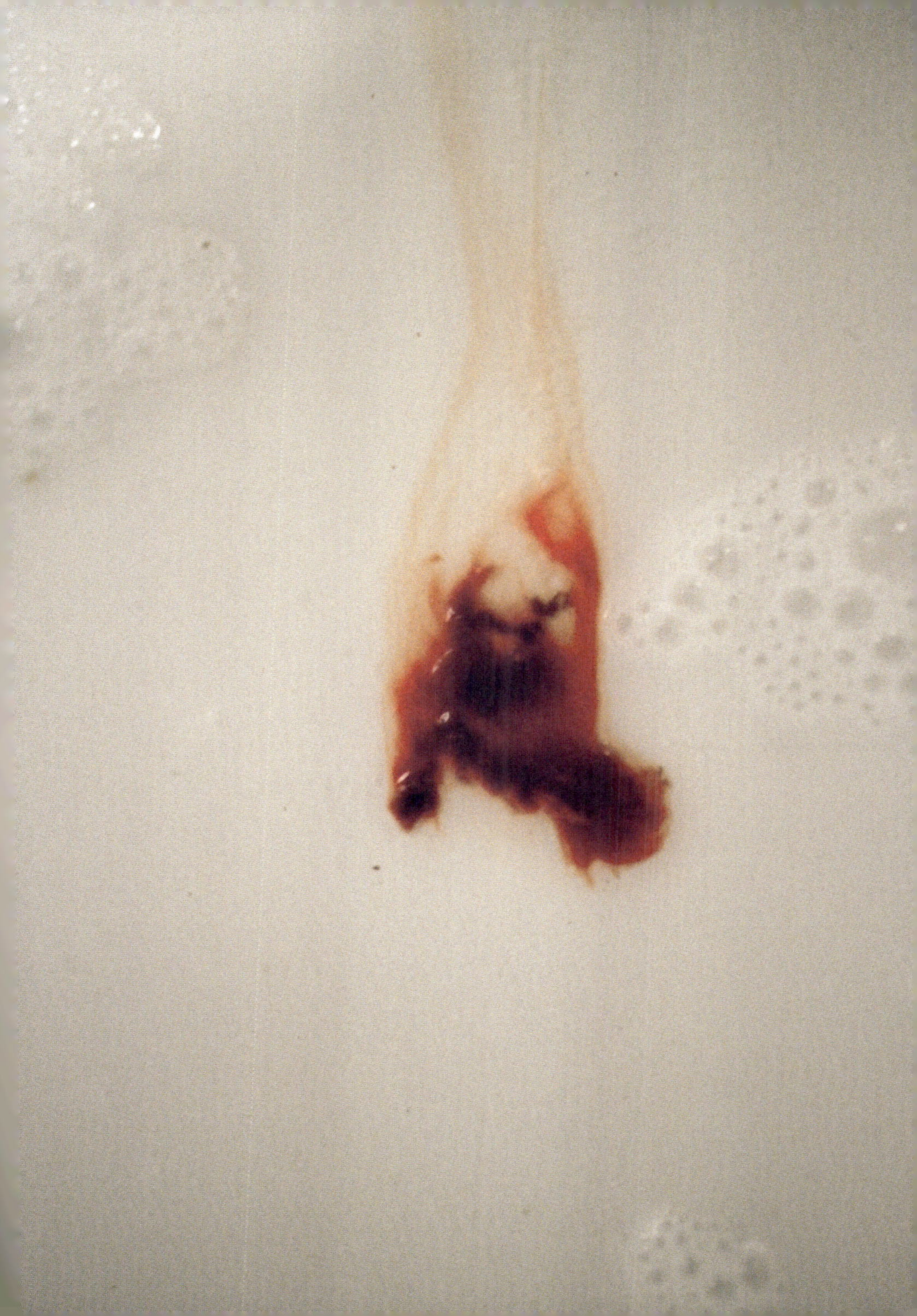

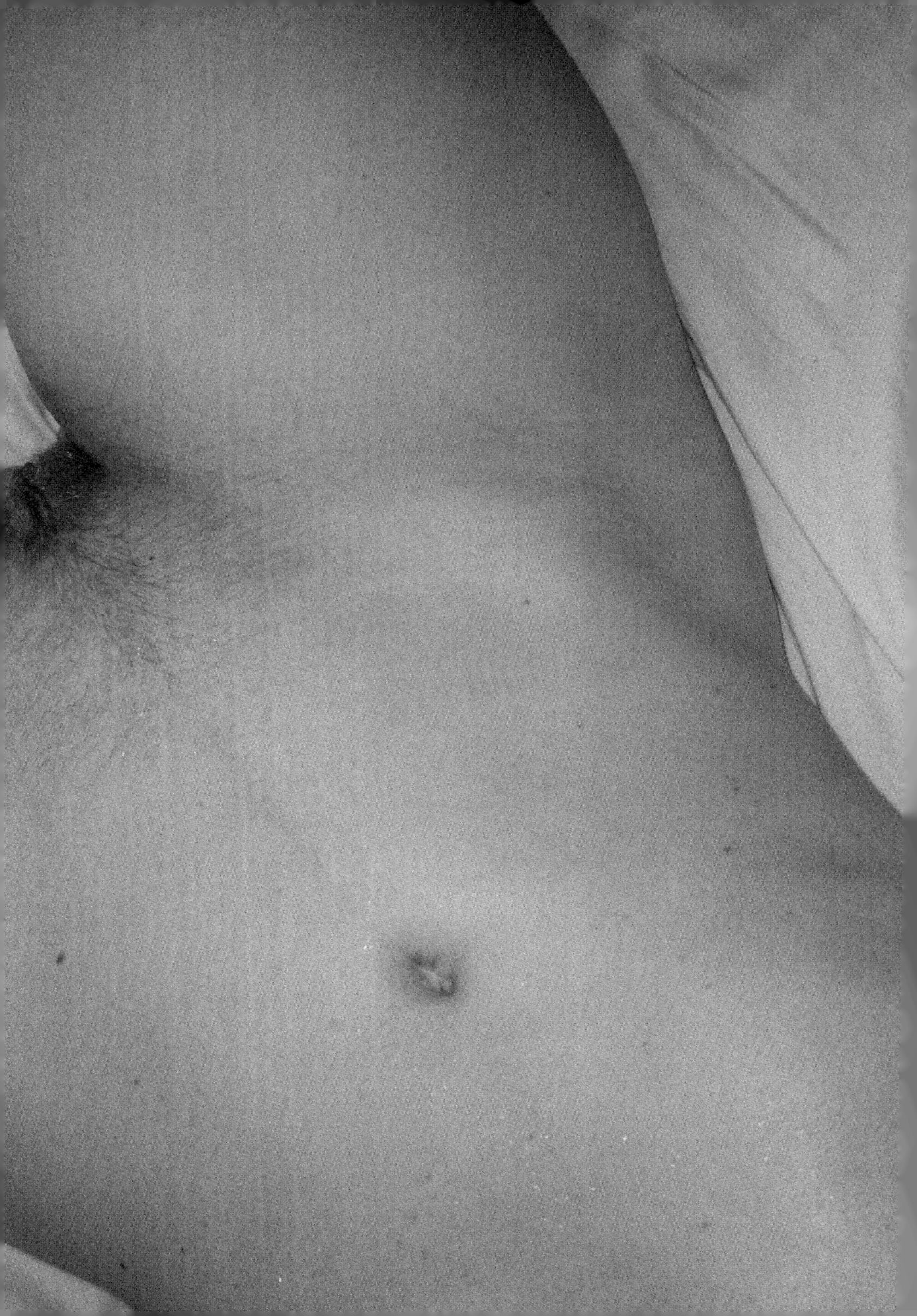

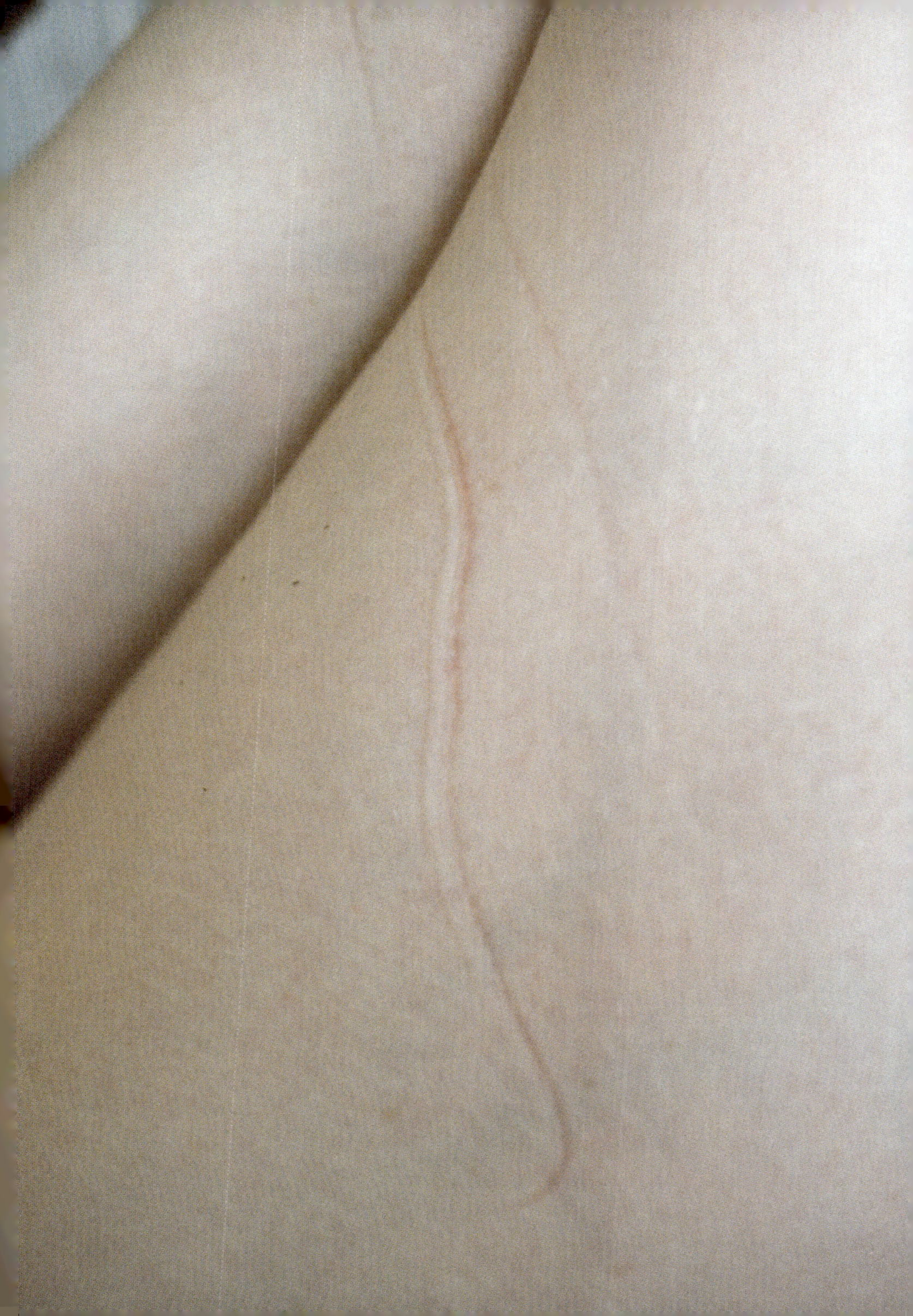

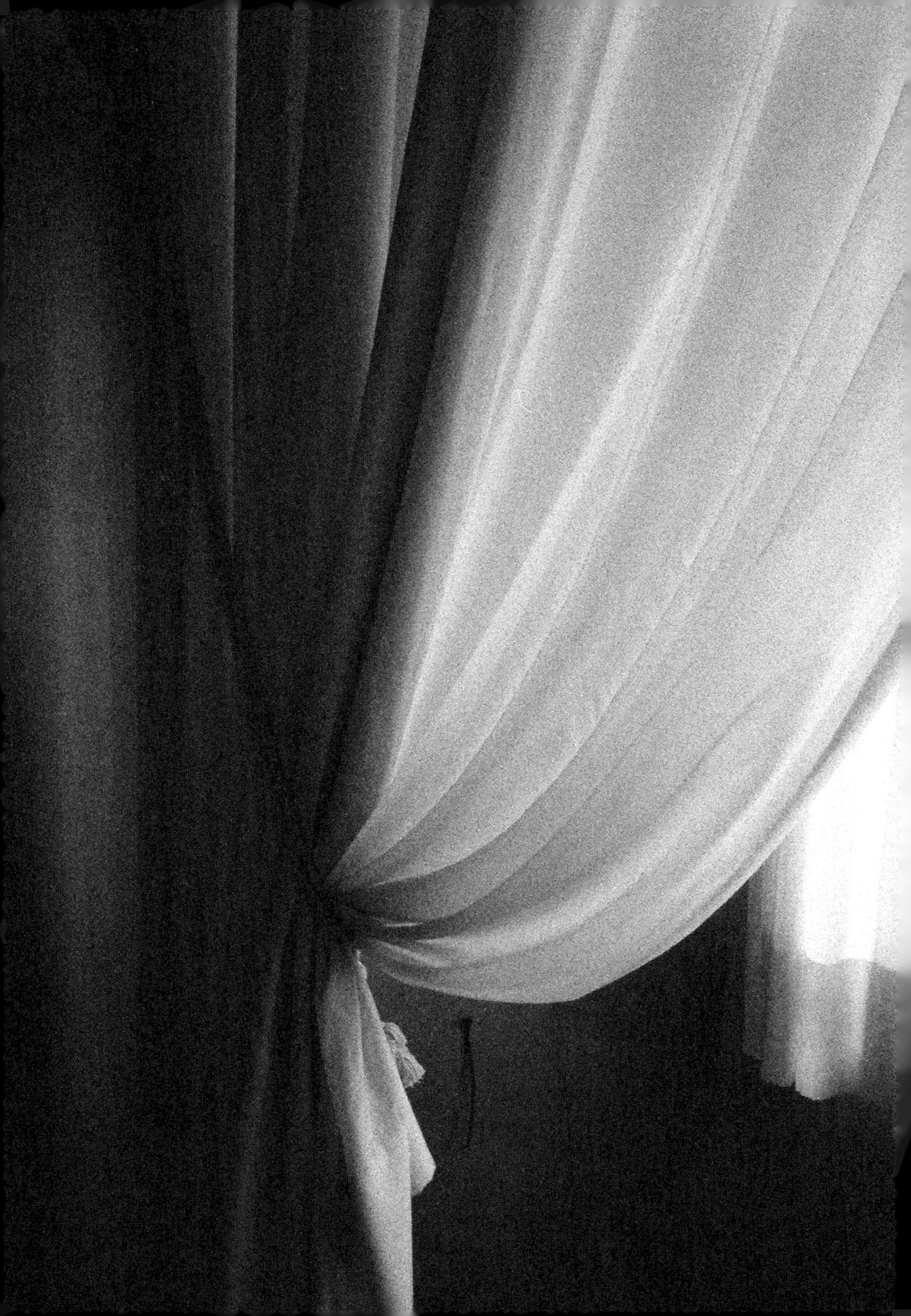

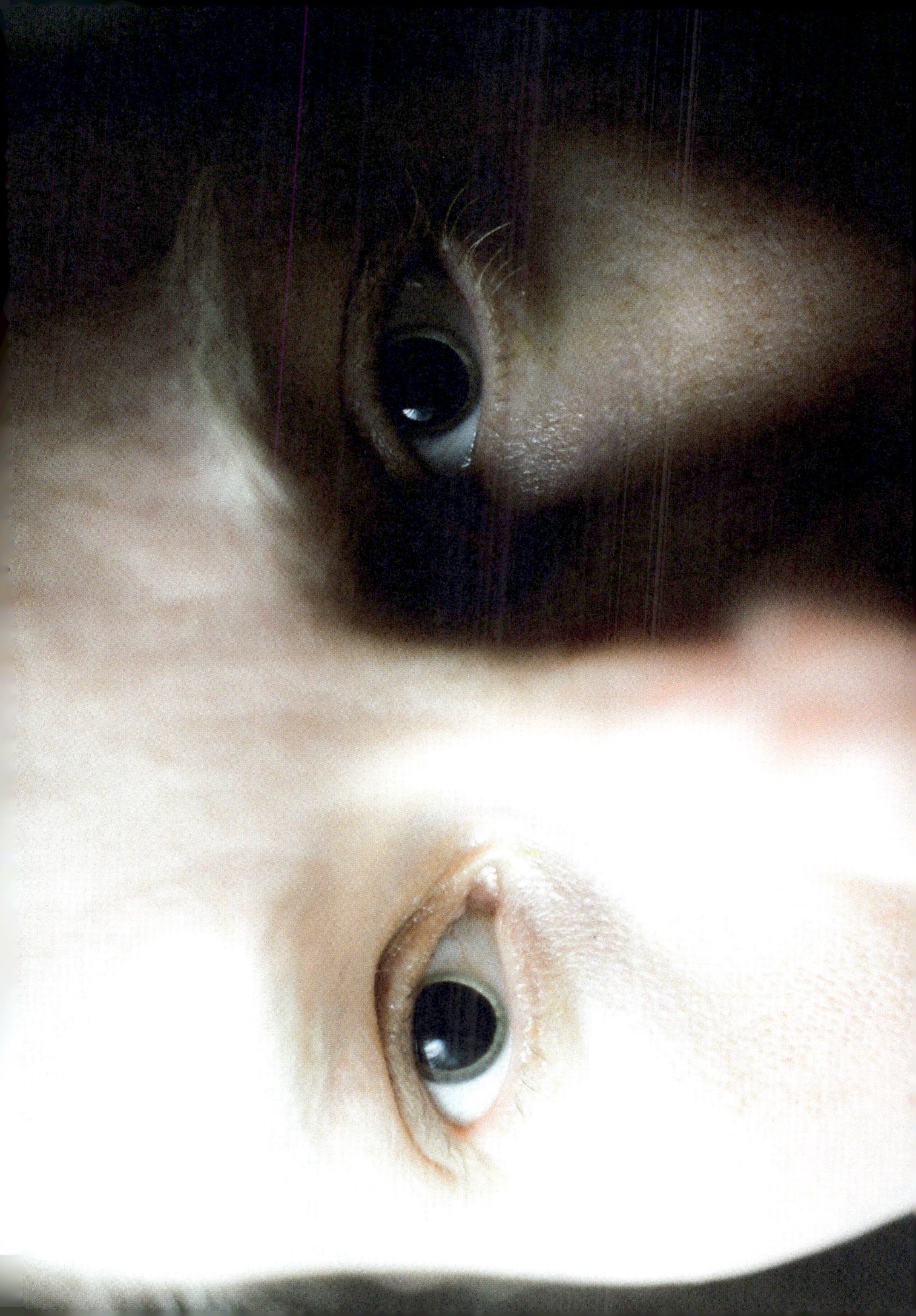

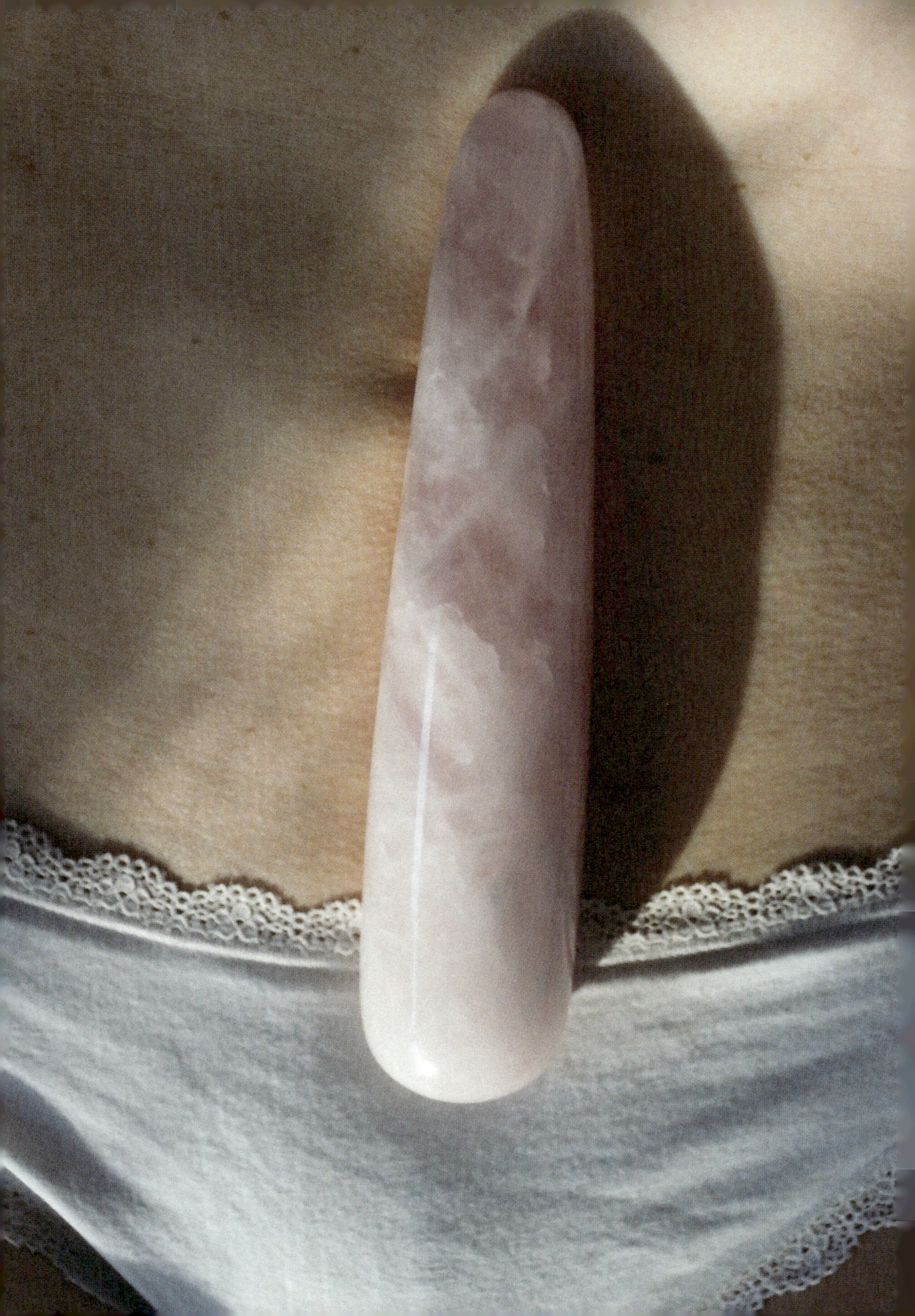

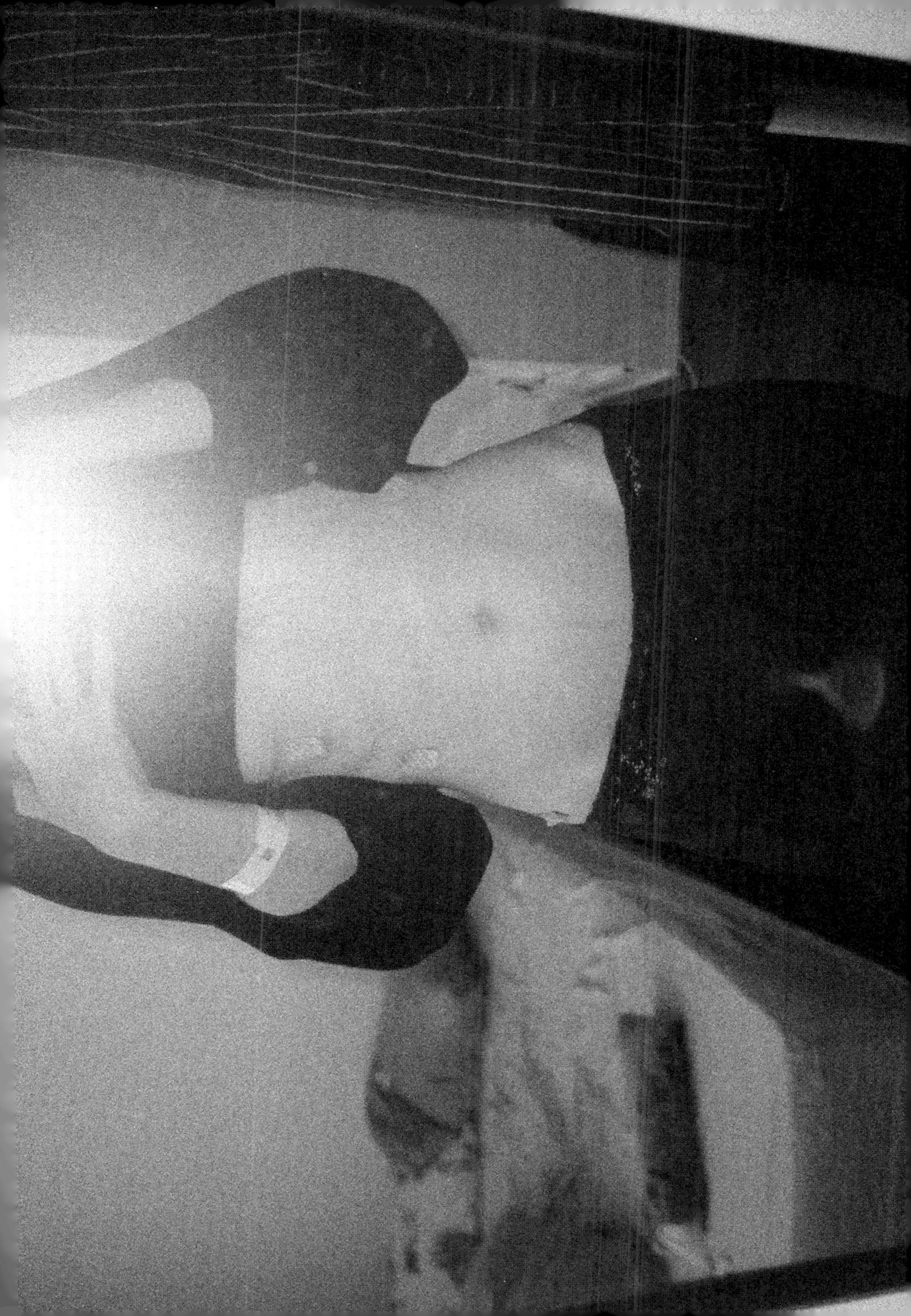

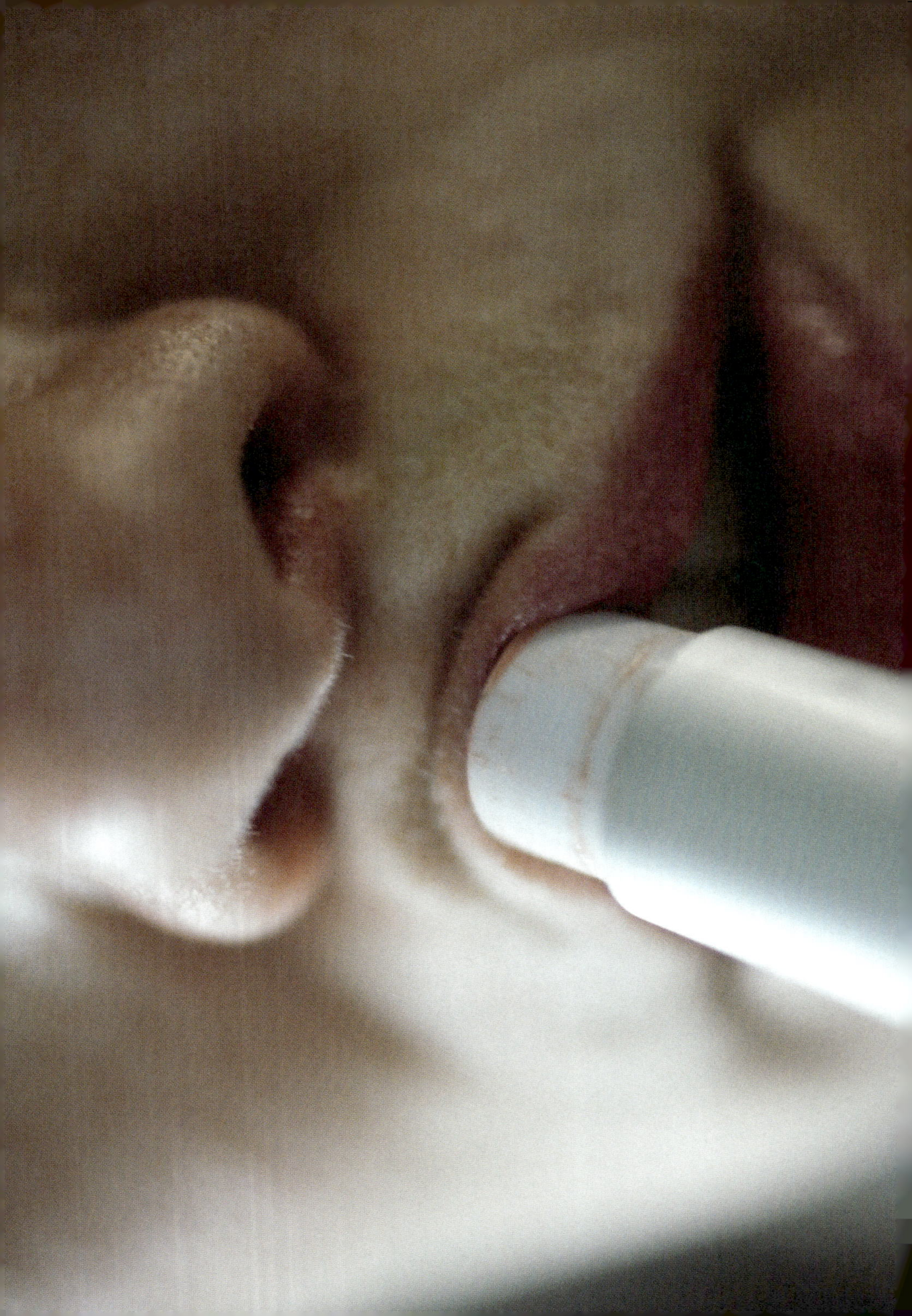

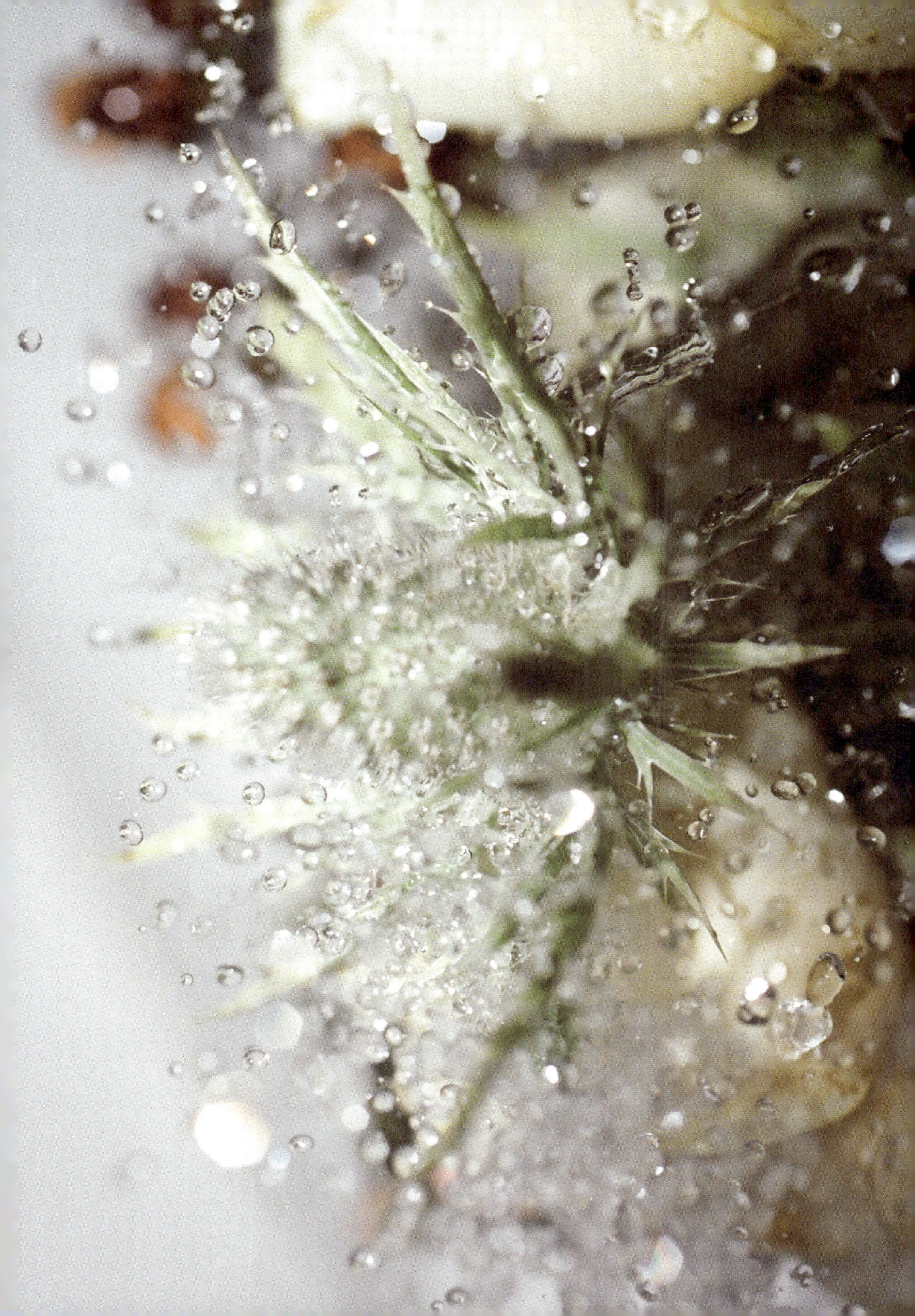

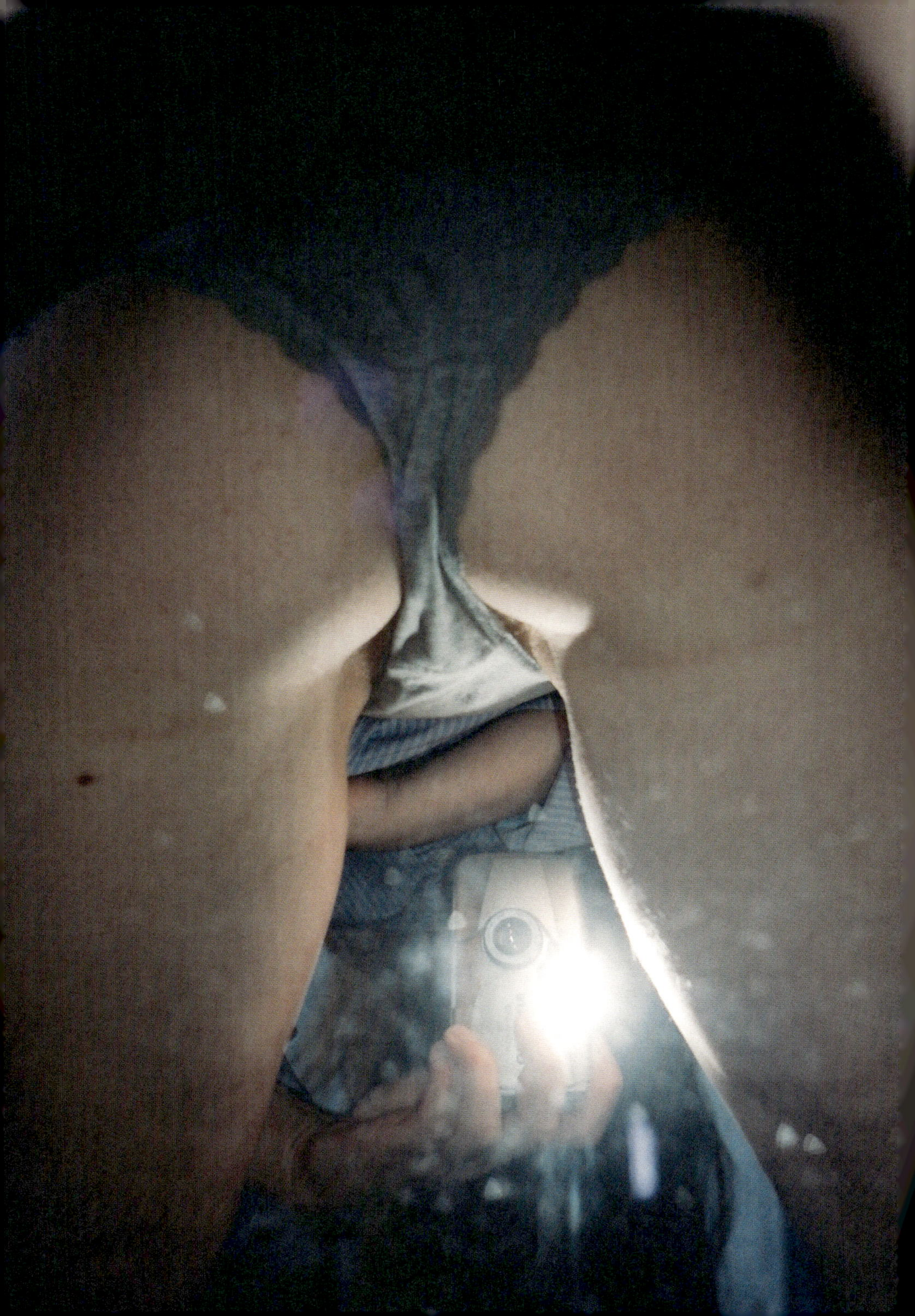

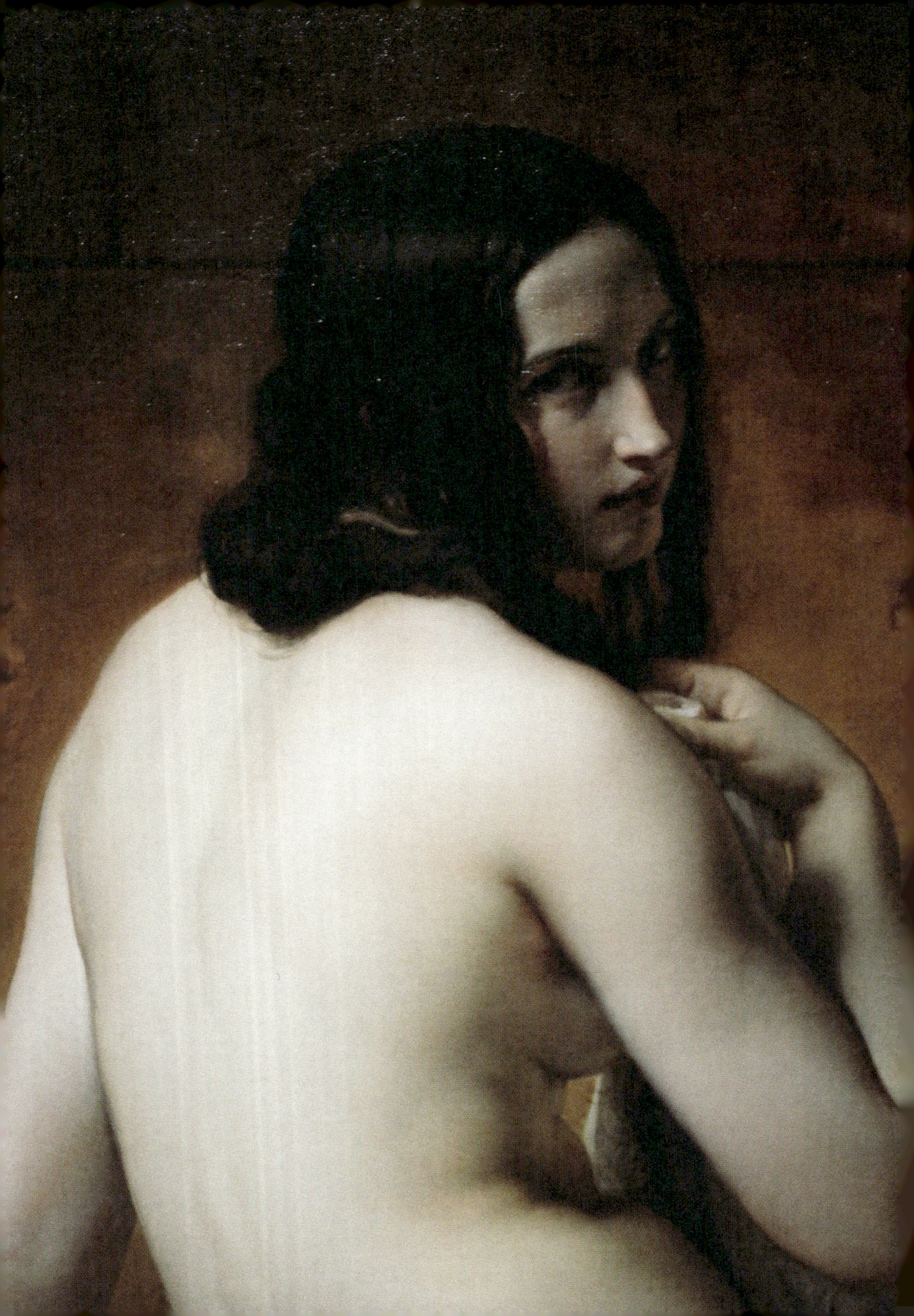

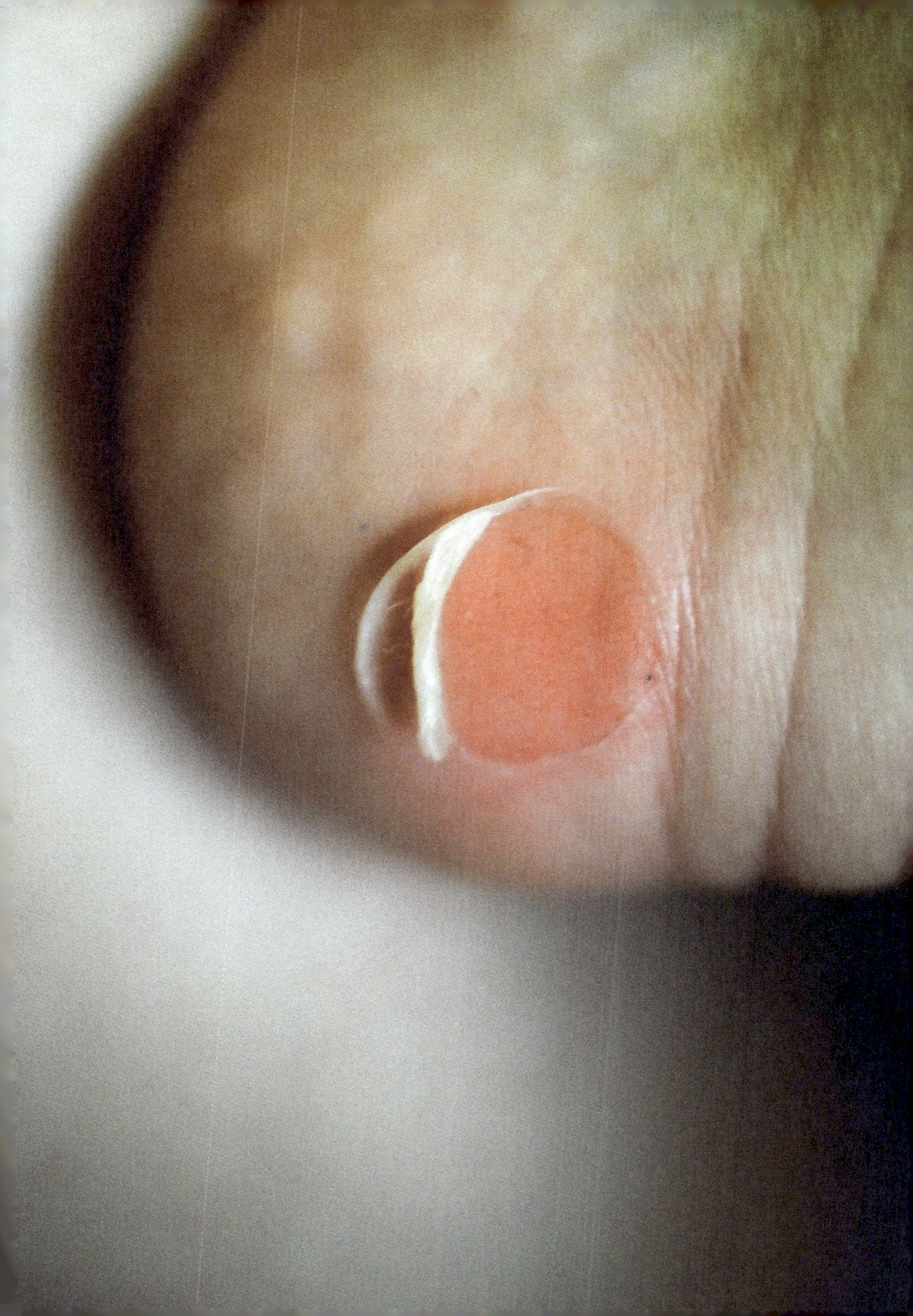

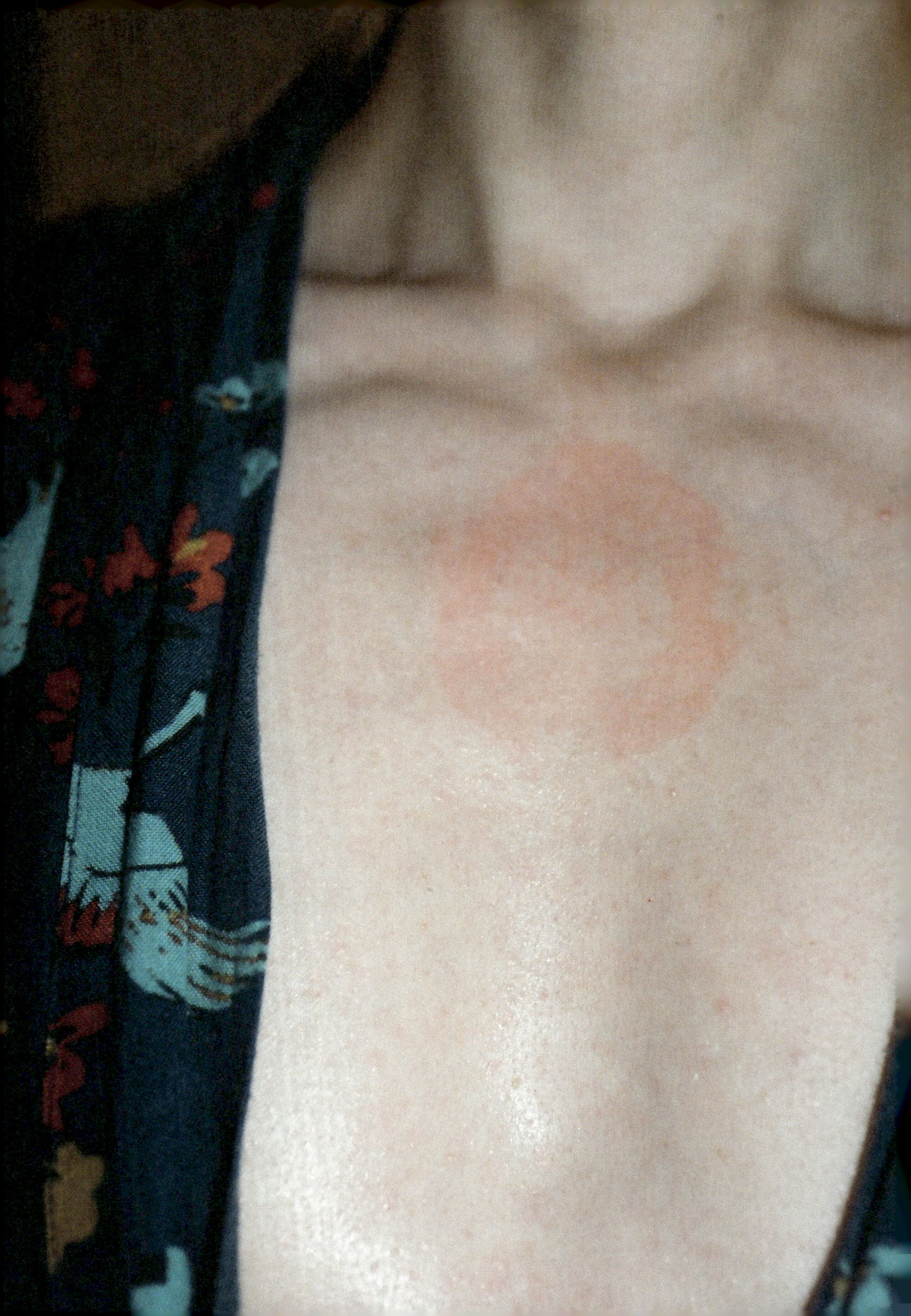

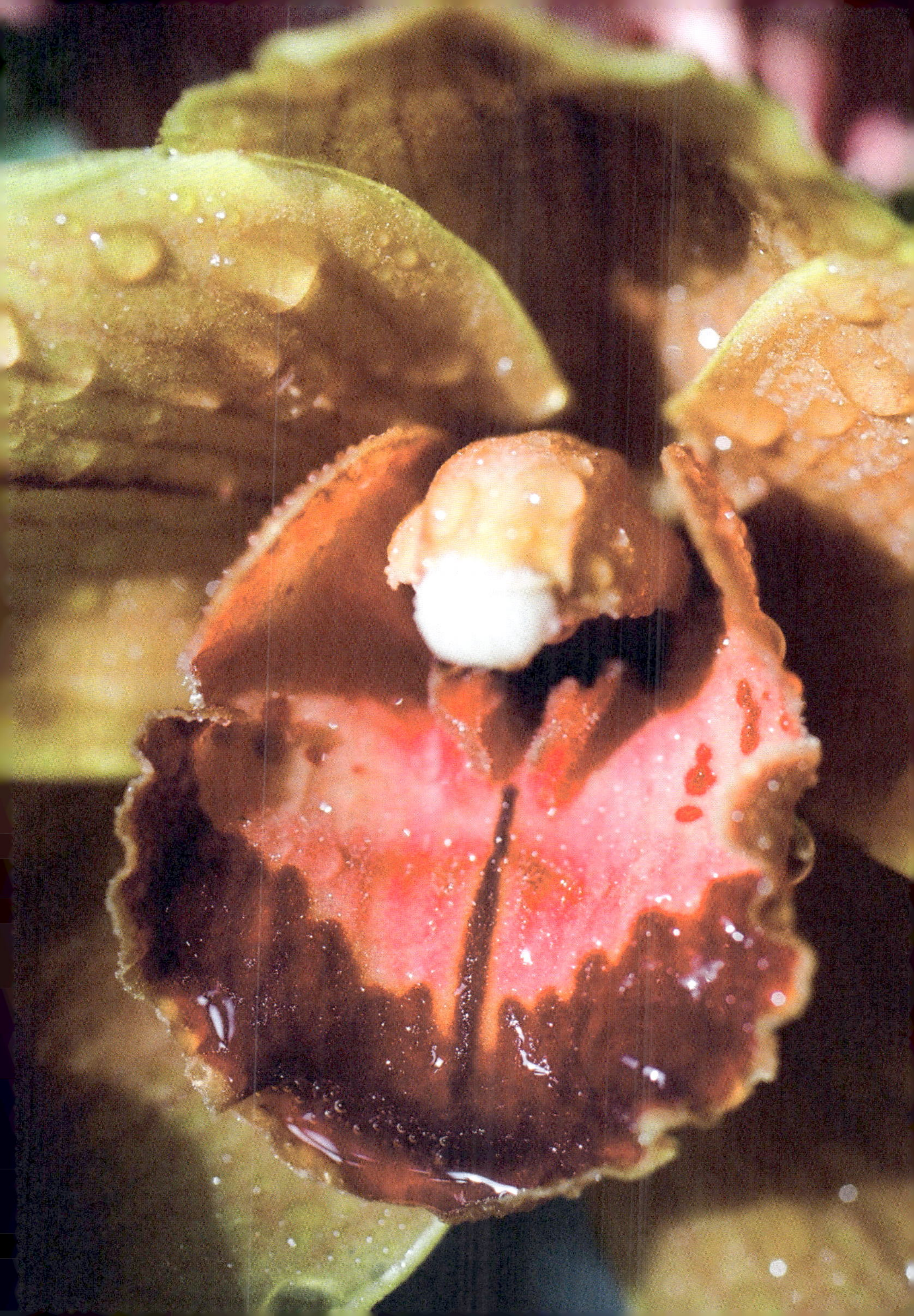

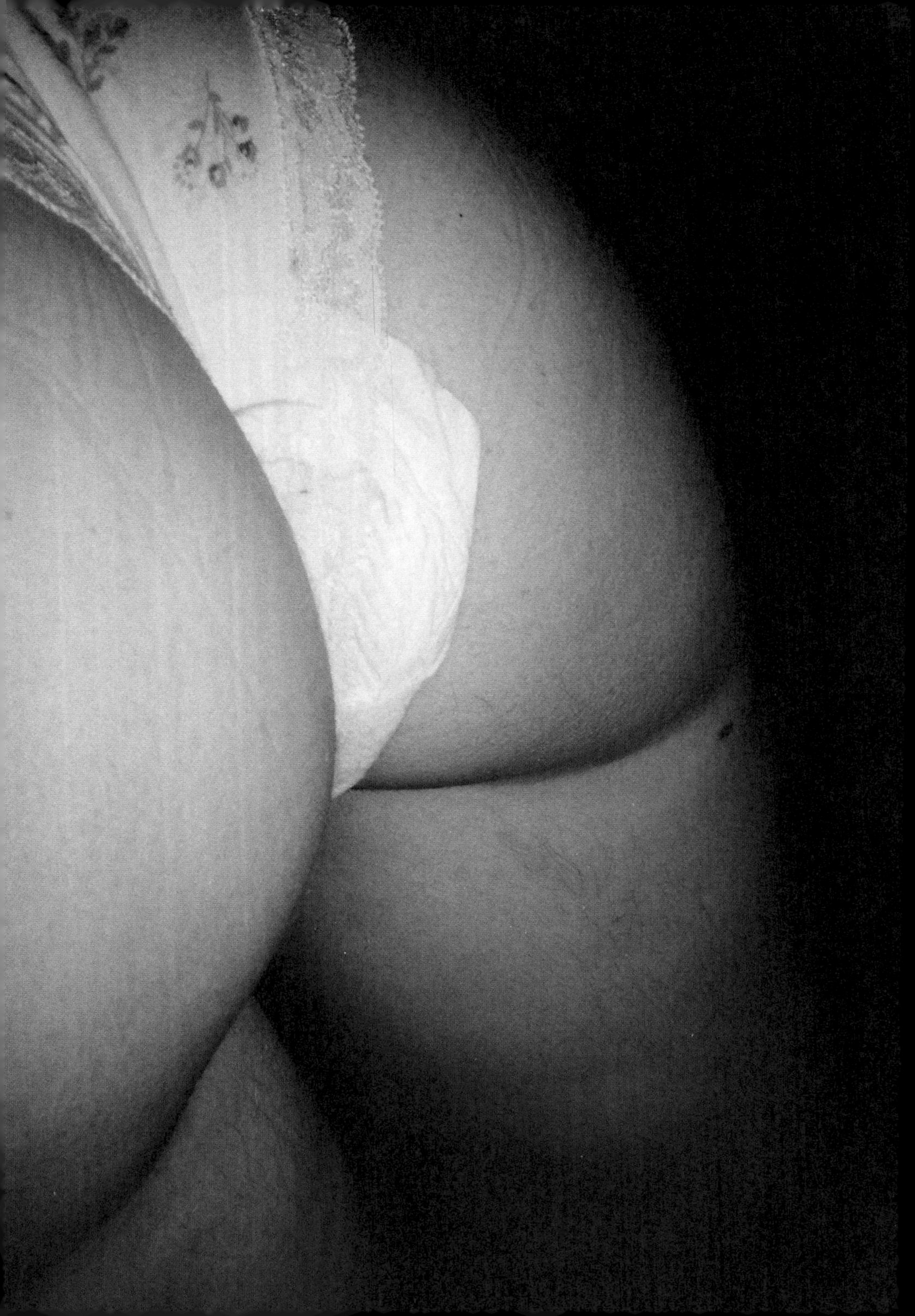

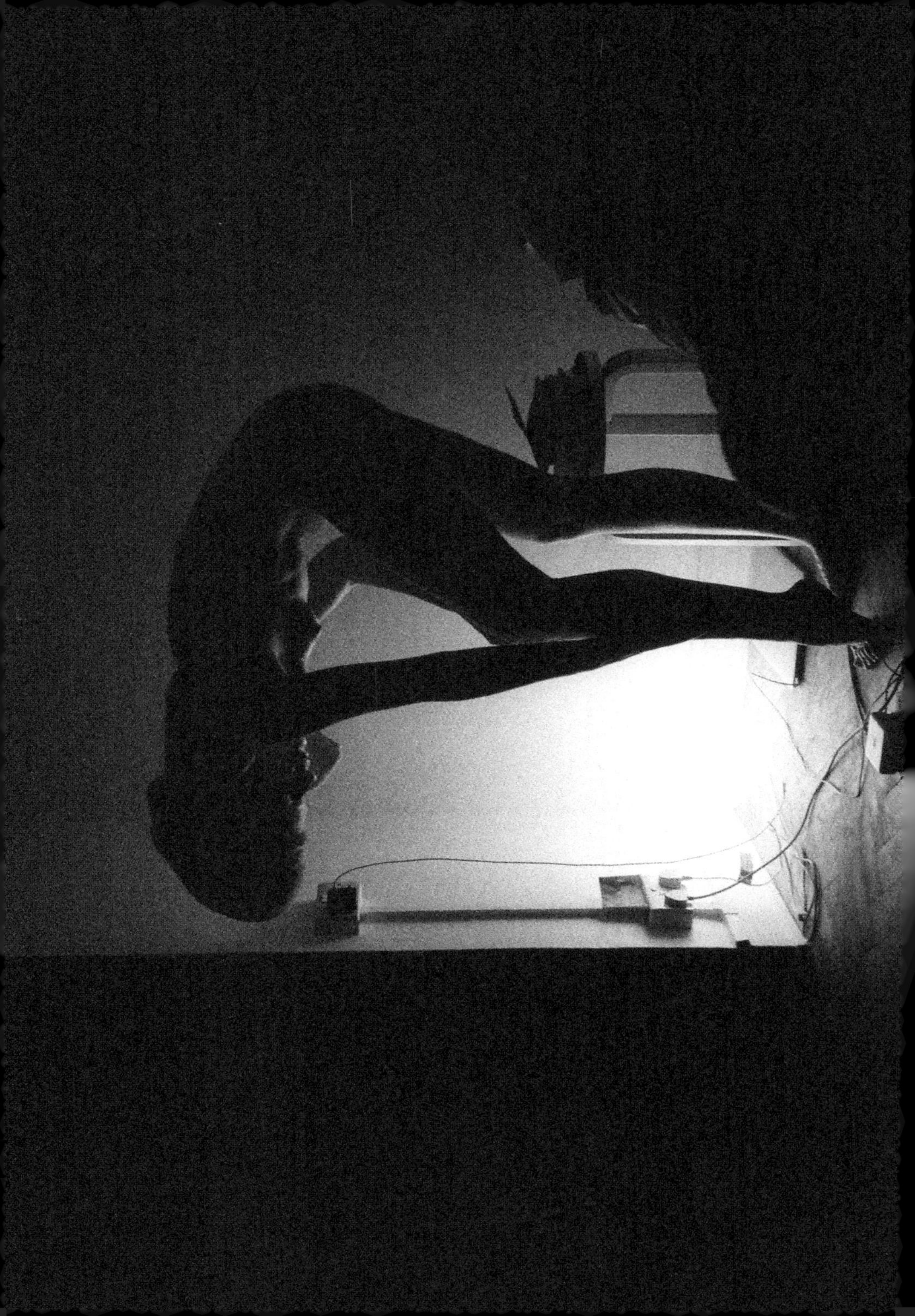

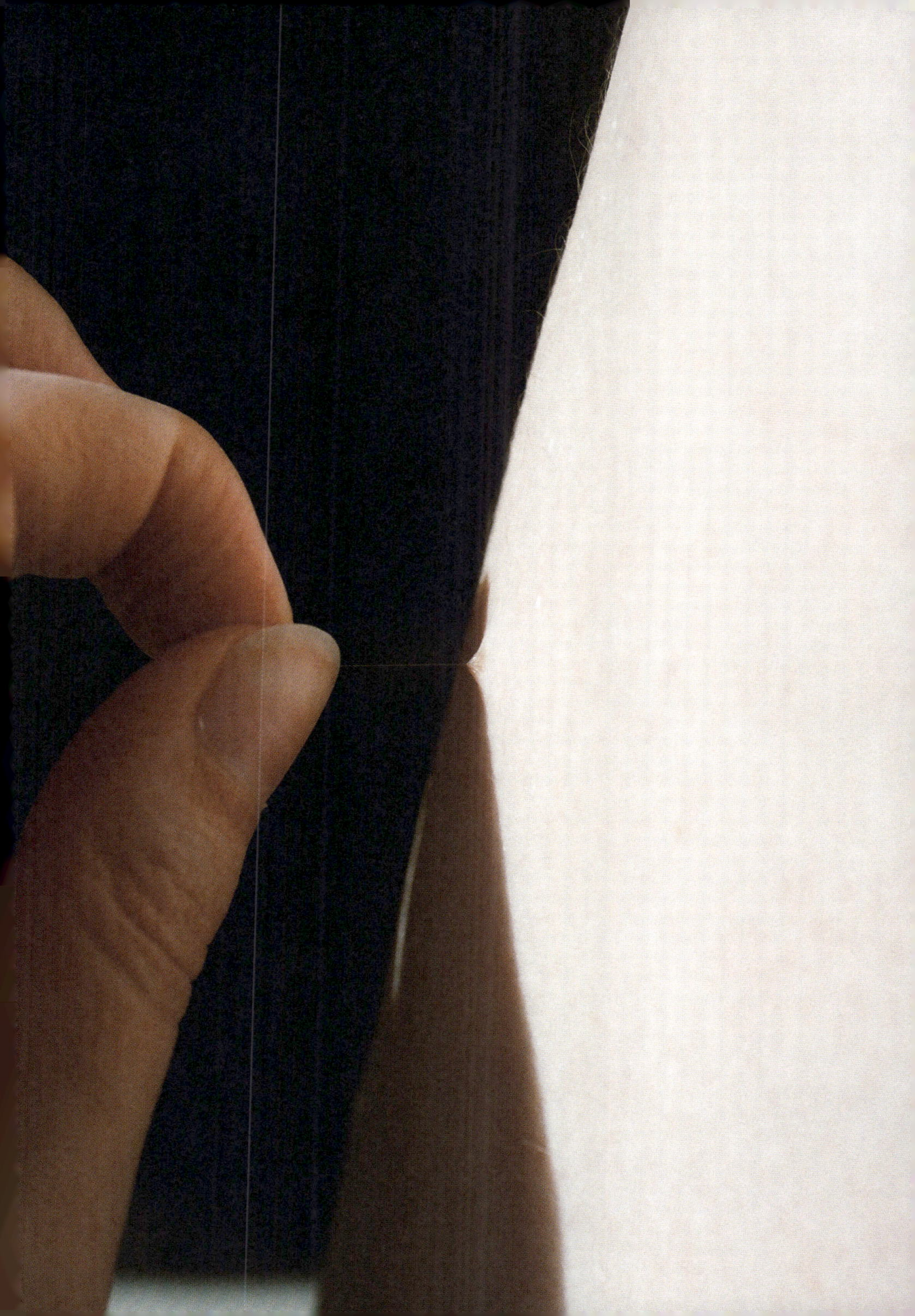

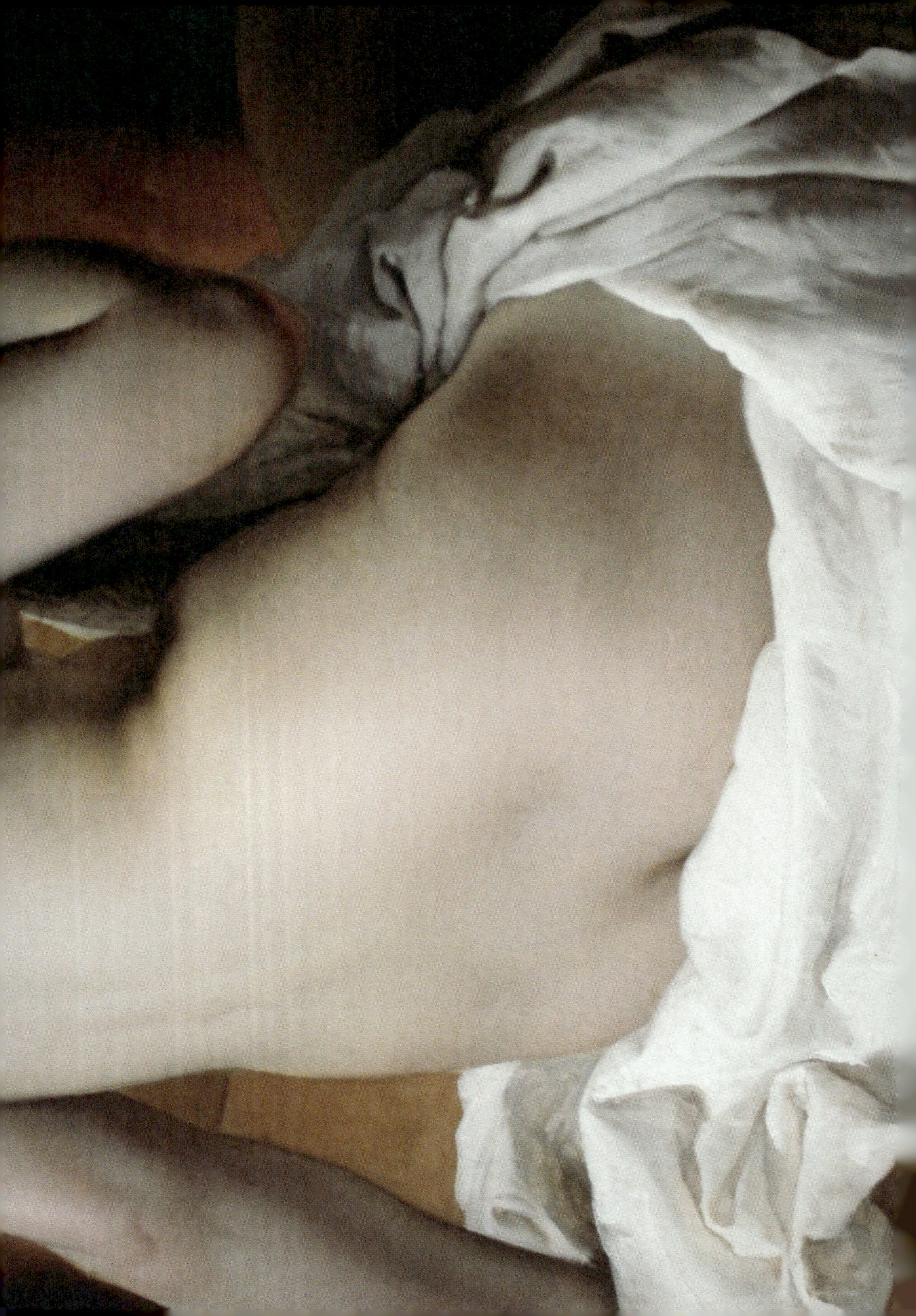

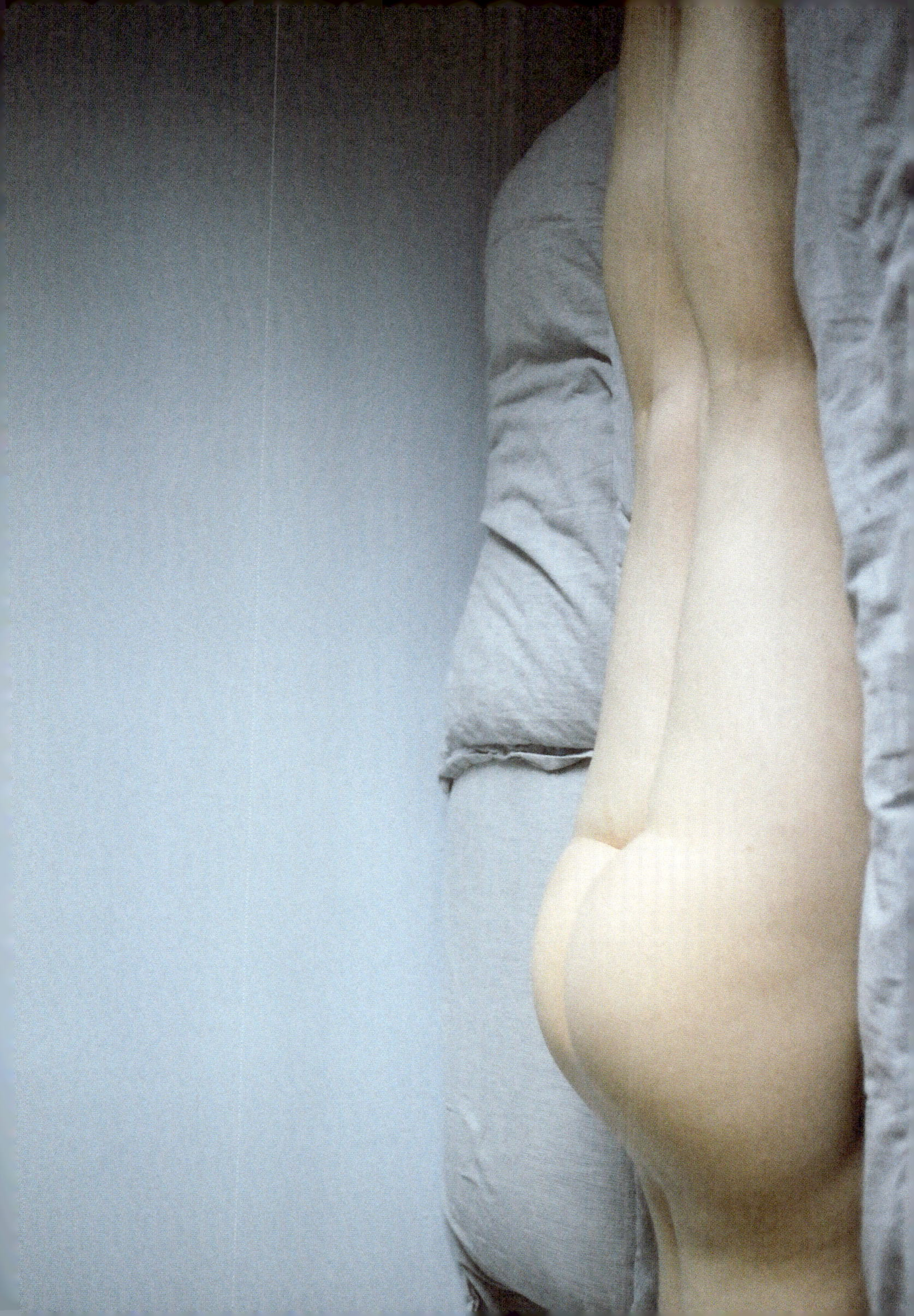

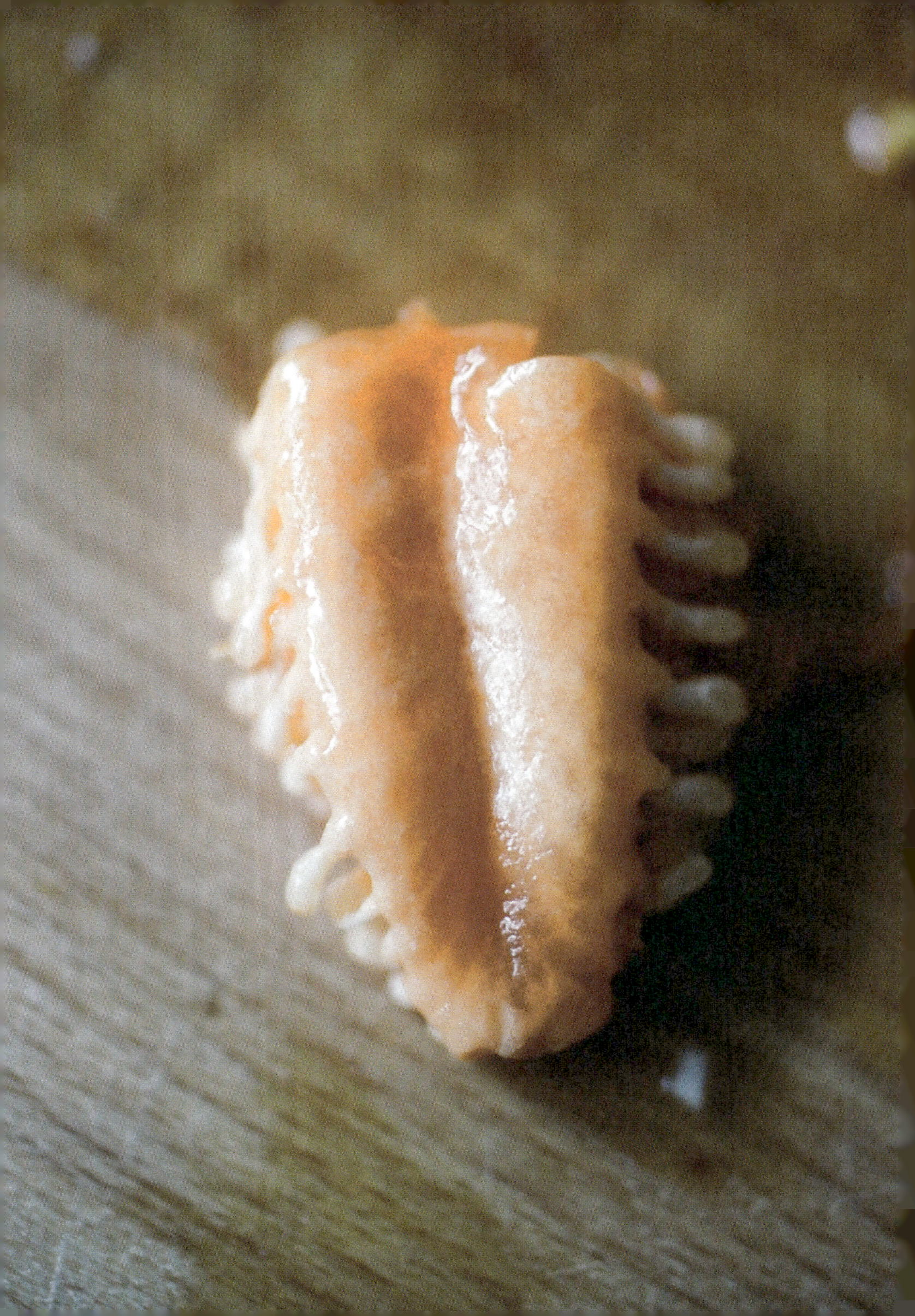

13

by Lina Scheynius
All photographs taken between 2019 and 2021

First edition of 1000
Published in November 2023
by David Desrimais, Lina Scheynius and Emma Zampieri

Legal deposit: December 2023
ISBN 978-2-36568-081-3
Printed in Lithuania

JBE Books
90 rue de la Folie-Méricourt
75011 Paris
jbe-books.com